Heart of Flame

Portrait of Katherine Mansfield, by Anne Rice, Cornwall, 1918. KM's red silk Indian shawl, embroidered with stylized flowers, is draped behind her. The shawl is in the Bibliothèque Municipale, Menton.
Te Papa (1940-0009-1)

ANNE CAME EARLY & began the great painting – me in that red, brick red frock with flowers everywhere. It's awfully interesting even now. … I painted her in my fashion as she painted me in hers. Her eyes …'little blue flowers plucked this morning' …
Letter to JMM, from Cornwall, 17 June 1918

SUDDENLY, THIS AFTERNOON, as I was thinking of you there flashed across my inward eye a beautiful poppy that we stood looking at in the garden of the Headland Hotel, Looe [in Cornwall]. Do you remember that marvellous black sheen at the base of the petal and the big purplish centre?
Letter to Anne Rice, Chalet des Sapins, Montana-sur-Sierre, Switzerland, 24 December 1921

Heart of Flame
KATHERINE MANSFIELD'S FLOWERS & TREES

COMPILER
Beverley Randell

Beverley Randell

ARTIST
Jenni Shoesmith

Strange flowers half opened, scarlet
Show me your heart of flame …

from Scarlet Tulips

STEELE ROBERTS
AOTEAROA

© illustrations Jenni Shoesmith 2020

A note on Katherine Mansfield's text — There are many different versions of KM's writing. We have generally attempted to follow the most recent and authoritative editions. We have silently corrected missing apostrophes — for instance, *I'll* for *Ill, it's* for *its, we'd* for *wed*. In general we have retained KM's random use of and/&, and have dealt with erratic hyphenation (e.g. zig zag/zig-zag/zigzag) case by case. Variant spellings have mostly been left intact (e.g. freezias, cosmias, toi-toi), but some other evident errors have been corrected (e.g. nasturium/nasturtium, miseltoe/mistletoe).

Acknowledgements — We thank all writers, editors and publishers whose books are listed on page 112. The meticulous transcriptions of Katherine Mansfield's work by Gerri Kimber, Vincent O'Sullivan, Anna Plumridge and the indefatigable Margaret Scott were invaluable.

Thanks to Sarah Bolland, Cherie Jacobson, Christine Ling, Mary Morris, Lynn Peck, Peter Sergel, Rosemary Steele and Quentin Wilson for editorial and design assistance.

Abbreviations — KM: Katherine Mansfield; JMM: John Middleton Murry.

ISBN 978-1-99-000716-3

STEELE ROBERTS AOTEAROA PUBLISHERS
Box 33555, Petone, Aotearoa New Zealand 5045
info@steeleroberts.co.nz • www.steeleroberts.co.nz

Contents

Introduction 7

I Deeply loved flowers 9
II Earliest memories 26
III Ablaze in Wellington gardens 37
IV The bright flowers of Europe 48
V Wild and windy Wellington 65
VI Away to the bush gloried hills 73
VII England through the seasons 83
VIII The warm, fragrant Mediterranean 94

APPENDICES

1 The influence of *Elizabeth and her German Garden* 108
2 KM's flowers today — Katherine Mansfield House & Garden in Wellington, and the Mansfield Garden at Hamilton Gardens 110

BIBLIOGRAPHY 112

INDEX OF PLANTS 113

COMPILER AND ARTIST 116

Katherine Mansfield at the Villa Isola Bella at Menton, France.
The plants in the foreground are pelargoniums.
Alexander Turnbull Library 1/2-011913-F

Introduction

I love flowers more than people …

Katherine Mansfield — KM — moved around a great deal in her short life, and wherever she stayed she observed flowers with a fresh eye and reacted to them with intense feeling. She adored scents and vivid, blazing colours. One of her characters said that a flower seller:

> took out and shook, and held up to the critical light bunch after bunch of round, bright flowers … purple and white violets that one longed not only to smell but to press against one's lips and almost to eat. Oh! how she loved flowers! What a passion she had for them and how much they meant to her. Yes, they meant almost everything. (*Notebook 38*)

To describe anemones, tulips and clematis KM used sensual language:

> seductive … kiss your silken petals … tremulous passion … rapture …

Ever since she was a small child, KM (born Kathleen Mansfield Beauchamp on 14 October 1888) cared greatly about flowers. She observed each one closely and often chose exactly the right words for them: 'Every daisy in the grass below has a starched frill.' Freesia leaves were 'light spears of green that criss-crossed over the flowers.' Toetoe was 'waving in the wind & looking for all the world like a family of little girls drying their hair.' Passion flowers were 'like white shells afloat'. The pelargonium had 'velvet eyes and leaves like moths' wings'.

KM occasionally confused pairs of similar names, but the plants she was describing can be identified by the precision of her words. The great thorny succulent plant in *Prelude* is still sometimes misnamed the American aloe, but it does not belong to the aloe family. It is the American agave (*Agave americana*). Japanese sunflowers are huge

American agave.

with nothing tiny about them — however, the words 'tiny jungle' are a perfect match for ground-covering Japanese windflowers (*Anemone hupehensis*). And in the vignette *It was late afternoon*, the puzzling plant with 'little sponge-like fruits' is misnamed mock orange: the name should have been orange-ball tree (*Buddleja globosa*).

The plants illustrated on the following pages are grouped, each connected to a particular place (or, in Chapter 1, 'Deeply loved flowers', to people).

Katherine Mansfield at the Villa Isola Bella.
Alexander Turnbull Library 1/2-011914-F

The amount of minute and delicate joy I get out of watching people and things when I am alone is simply enormous ... Just the same applies to my feelings for what is called 'nature'. Other people won't stop and look at the things I want to look at ... it's enormously valuable and marvellous when I'm alone, the detail of life, the *life* of life.

The Katherine Mansfield Notebooks, Volume Two, page 56

I

Deeply loved flowers

Primroses! Oh, what wouldn't I give for some flowers. Oh Brett – this longing for flowers. I *crave* them. I think of them – of the feeling of tulips' stems and petals, of the touch of violets and the light on marigolds & the smell of wall flowers. No, it does not bear writing about. I could kiss the earth that bears flowers. Alas, I love them far TOO much!

Letter to Dorothy Brett, Chalet des Sapins, Montana-sur-Sierre, Switzerland, 22 December 1921

A few special flowers had lifelong significance for KM. Her friend Ida Baker ('Lesley Moore') in *Memories of Katherine Mansfield by LM*, recalled some of KM's reactions, writing, 'For years the scent and sight of lilac brought back some deep emotional experience for her'. KM appreciated wild flowers and wrote that the 'rather meagre beauty' of her London garden in the spring had been 'reinforced by nine immense dandelions'. Ida, regarding them as weeds, destroyed one, and never forgot KM's wail of distress. In 1923 Ida would drop similar flowers — much-loved marigolds — onto Katherine's coffin.

Wild buttercups and daisies were poignant reminders of the New Zealand childhood KM had shared with her young brother Leslie ('Bogey') who was killed in Belgium in 1915, aged 21.

She adored violets and roses all her life, and her husband Jack loved anemones. KM wrote that a witness at her wedding to John Middleton Murry in 1918 had arrived 'like some delightful bird who had flown in laughing through the bright anemone flowers.'

French marigold.

VIOLET *Viola odorata*

SHE WANTED to make a surprise for the grandmother … First she would put a leaf inside [a matchbox] with a big violet lying on it, then she would put a very small white picotee, perhaps, on each side of the violet, and then she would sprinkle some lavender on the top, but not to cover their heads.

She often made these surprises for the grandmother, and they were always most successful.
Prelude, VI

THE FLOWER SELLER … took out … bunch after bunch of round, bright flowers. Jonquils and anemones, roses and marigolds, plumes of mimosa, lilies-of-the-valley in a bed of wool, stocks, a strange pink like the eyes of white rabbits, and purple and white violets that one longed not only to smell but to press against one's lips and almost to eat. Oh! how she loved flowers! What a passion she had for them and how much they meant to her. Yes, they meant almost everything.

… And the crowning joy and wonder [was] that she was perfectly free to look at them, to 'take them in' for just as long as she liked … For the first time she drank a long heady draft of this new wine, freedom. There was no-one at her elbow to say: 'But my dear, this is not the moment to rave about flowers', no-one to tell her that hotel bedrooms were more important than marigolds … So, she drank the cup to the sweet dregs and bought an armful of mixed beauties and carried them into the café with her.
There is No Answer, Notebook 38 (Notebooks, Volume Two)

ALL THE FLORISTS' WINDOWS are full of the blue light of violets. And I can't resist them – tight posies tied with yellow flax – *Do* you feel flowers like this – a sense of complete magic – I am spellbound – entranced.
Letter to Vera Beauchamp, Wellington, 12 June 1908

I WENT TO THE FLOWER MARKET and stood among the buyers and bought wholesale you know, at the auction in a state of a lively terrified joy 3 dozen rose buds and 6 bunches of violets.
Letter to JMM, Bandol, France, 30-31 December 1915

… HOW I *adored* Life & *dreaded* Death. I'd like to write my books & spend some happy time with Jack (not very much faith in that) and see Lawrence in a sunny place & pick violets – all kinds of flowers. Oh, I'd like to do heaps of things really, but I don't mind if I do not do them.
The Walking Stick, Notebook 26 (Notebooks, Volume Two), 17 December 1919

THE FLOWERS ARRIVED in the most perfect condition – so fresh they might have been gathered ½ an hour ago. I have made a most exquisite 'garden' of the moss, little violet roots, anemone roots & crocus blades. It's like a small world. The rest are in a jug. They are supremely lovely flowers. But please do something for me. I *beg* you. Tell me (1) where they grew (2) how they grew (3) was there snow near (4) what kind of a day was it (5) were they among other flowers or are they the first? Don't bother about description. I only want *fact*. In fact if you can send me a kind of weather & 'aspects' report as near as you can you would earn my deep deep gratitude. By aspects I mean the external face of nature.
Letter to Ida Baker, Paris, 24 April 1922

THE ROOM is full of violets –
And yet there's but this little bowl
Of blossoms on the mantel-piece.
Violets

> If she only had sixpence left for a meal, the bunch of violets for the table would come first.
> *KM's remark to her friend Margaret Wishart in 1908*
> *(in Antony Alpers' 1954 biography of KM)*

LILAC *Syringa vulgaris*

IT IS LOVELY in the public gardens; it is full spring. The lilac is in flower …
& the new grass quivers in the light, & the trees, their delicate leaves gold in
the sun, stand with branches outspread as if in blessing …
There are certain human beings on this earth … Unbound papers

FROM EARLY MORNING the lilac tosses its beautiful plumes and the scent –
which is the very quintessence of Spring – floats like a pale mist across the
lawn over the garden, and in through the muslin curtains …
The Thoughtful Child and the Lilac Tree

… DIM MIST of a fog-bound day,
From the lilac trees that droop in St Mary's Square
The dead leaves fall, a silent, fluttering crowd.
Dead thoughts that, shivering, fall on the barren earth …
… Over and under it all the muttering murmur of London.
October (To V.M.B.)

YOU COULD NOT see a leaf on the syringa bushes for the white clusters.
Prelude, VI

IT IS VERY WARM today. All the windows are wide open. From early morning people have passed along the quai carrying lilac … little stout men, the bunch upside down, looped to a finger by a knotted string – young girls carrying it along the arm – little children with their faces quite buried – and old fat women clasping the branches – just a frill of flower showing above their bosoms.

… we drew up alongside a hospital train. From my window I could see into the saloon. There were pallet beds round the walls – the men covered to the chin never moved an inch … All round the walls of the car kind female hands had placed big bunches of purple and white lilac. What lovely lilac! said the people in the train with me. 'Look! Look how fine it is!'
Letter to JMM, Paris, 6-7 May 1915

*the scent – which is the very quintessence of Spring –
floats like a pale mist across the lawn*

THE BRANCHES of the lilac tree
Are bent with blossom – in the air
They sway and languish dreamily
And we, pressed close, are kissing there
The blossoms falling on her hair –
Oh, lilac tree, Oh, lilac tree
Shelter us, cover us, secretly.
The Lilac Tree

MY THOUGHTS *flew* to you
immediately the guns sounded
[for Armistice Day]. I opened the
window and it really *did* seem –
just in those first few moments that
a wonderful change happened
… and I saw that in our garden
the lilac bush had believed in
the South wind & was covered in
buds – – –
   I thought of my brother and of
you. And I longed to embrace you
both …
Letter to Ottoline Morrell, Hampstead,
17 November 1918

THERE WAS NO SOUND in the house any more, nor any light
except the white beams of moonlight shining on the carpets […] the flowers
that were yesterday night in the garden, the hydrangeas, the silvery waxy
branches of syringa flowers, the red roses that grew singly on long stems &
the little round roses that fluttered their petals on to the grass at a breath.
Serene & majestic stood the house, filled with its brood of slecping people.
The air blew through it, lifting the curtains & filling it with the scent of the
earth and grass and trees.
Hydrangeas, Notebook 10 (Notebooks, Volume One)

DOG (OX-EYE) DAISY *Leucanthemum vulgare*

A BEAUTIFUL daisy pied creek
Urewera Notebook (Te Pohue)

EACH TIME I take up my pen *you* are with me, you are mine. You are my playfellow, my brother, & we shall range all over our country together … I do not write alone. That every word I write & every place I visit I carry you with me. Indeed that might be the motto of my book. There are daisies on the table and a red flower, like a poppy, shines through. Of daisies I will write, of the dark, of the wind – & the sun & the mists, of wharves – ah! of all that you loved & that I too love and feel.
Notebook 34, 14 February 1916

HOW LOVELY the fields must be. I wish we were walking there – at our ease – those bright silver daisies are in flower and the sorrel is in feather – We should pause and admire and talk until suddenly I felt music come streaming down those great beams of sunlight & little trills, little shakes came from the flowers and the wind ran among the harp-like trees & the beauty of Life was almost too great to bear – I am sure if we were together we should be caught up to heaven in chariots of fire innumerable times.
Letter to Ottoline Morrell, Hampstead, 10 June 1919

VERY LARGE astonished daisies are beginning to flower everywhere – even in the gravel.
Letter to JMM, Ospedaletti, Italy, 15 October 1919

THE CLEANLINESS of Switzerland! Darling it is frightening. The chastity of my lily-white bed! The waxy-fine floors! The huge bouquet of white lilac, fresh, crisp from the laundry in my little salon! Every daisy in the grass below has a starched frill …
Letter to JMM, Switzerland, 7 May 1921

NOW IT'S DARK. The big daisies in the vase on the table have shut their pretty eyes – The shadows are wonderfully quiet – The sea sounds as though it were sweeping up hollow caves …
Letter to JMM, Ospedaletti, Italy, 17 October 1919

I WISH YOU COULD see this glass of flowers on the dining room table – daisies & roses. Field daisies, but larger than English ones, and very wide with the fringed petals dipped in *bright* crimson and crimson roses from the wild garden at the side of the steps. I have just gathered the third rose and remarked hundreds of buds will be blowing in a week or two.
Letter to JMM, Ospedaletti, Italy, 23 October 1919

AND HERE on the table are five daisies & an orchid that Pa picked for me & tied with a bit of grass & handed me. If I had much to forgive him I would forgive him much for this little bunch of flowers.
Letter to JMM, Ospedaletti, Italy, 12 November 1919

BEE ORCHID *Ophrys apifera*

OH, HOW BEAUTIFUL Life is, Virginia, it is marvellously beautiful. Were one to live for ever it would not be long enough. Sometimes I sit on the wall watching the sun & the wind shake over the long grass & the wild orchid cups & I feel – – – simply helpless before this wonder.
Letter to Virginia Woolf, Isola Bella, Menton, 27 December 1920

LAWN DAISY *Bellis perennis*
DANDELION *Taraxacum officinale*

THE LAWN is white with daisies – gold splashed with dandelions – but where the lilac tree lives there is a little doormat of mauve bloom, and the song of the brown bird has turned us into an enchanted family.
The Thoughtful Child and the Lilac Tree

> *Of daisies I will write, of the dark, of the wind –*
> *& the sun & the mists, of wharves – ah! of all*
> *that you loved & that I too love and feel.*

THEN THERE WERE Dinner Parties under the Fuchsia bush on the pink seat, when she'd do the cooking and make cakes of rich brown flour and water, and sliced geranium stalk for 'leming' peel. Truly it was easy to give dinner parties, the garden was so full of cooking things. Pepper in pepper pots at Mr Poppy's, Eggs – ready poached – at Mr Daisy's, and Caraway Seeds at Grandfather Dandelion's.
The Thoughtful Child

THE DINNER was baking beautifully on a concrete step. She began to lay the cloth on a pink garden seat. In front of each person she put two geranium leaf plates, a pine needle fork and a twig knife. There were three daisy heads on a laurel leaf for poached eggs, some slices of fuchsia petal cold beef, some lovely little rissoles made of earth and water and dandelion seeds, and the chocolate custard which she decided to serve in the pawa shell she had cooked it in.
Prelude, VIII; *'pawa' is paua.*

I AM TIRED, blissfully tired. Do you suppose that daisies feel blissfully tired when they shut for the night and the dews descend upon them?
Et in Arcadia Ego

SINCE THIS LITTLE ATTACK I've had a queer thing has happened. I feel that my love and longing for the external world – I mean the world of *nature* has suddenly increased a million times – when I think of the little flowers that grow in grass, and little streams and places where we can lie & look up at the clouds – Oh I simply *ache* for them – for them with you …
Letter to JMM, Bandol, France, 20 February 1918

THE TREES are trees again & one can face the light without shuddering. Garsington must be very lovely just now & your garden.

It has been a miracle to watch the roots & bulbs *buried* by M. last October burst out of their little graves and put on beauty – rather meagre London beauty – but reinforced by nine immense dandelions the garden is to a kind eye – quite gay …
Letter to Ottoline Morrell, Hampstead, 20 April 1919

SIX MOUNTAINS & then a soft still quiet valley where no wind blows – not even enough to fray the one o'clock dandelions …
Letter to JMM, Ospedaletti, Italy, 1 November 1919. 'One o'clock' refers to a children's game. If it takes one puff to blow all the seeds away, the time is one o'clock …

NOW THIS MORNING the mist is rolling up, wave on wave, and the pines & the firs, exquisitely clear, green and violet-blue show on the mountain sides. This grass, too, in the foreground, waving high, with one o'clocks like bubbles & flowering fruit trees like branches of pink & white coral …
Letter to JMM, Switzerland, 9 May 1921

BUTTERCUP *Ranunculus repens*

TO SIT IN FRONT of the little wood fire, your hands crossed in your lap and your eyes closed – to fancy you see again upon your eyelids all the dancing beauty of the day, to feel the flame on your throat as you used to imagine you felt the spot of yellow when Bogey [Leslie Beauchamp] held a buttercup under your chin …
Et in Arcadia Ego

THEY BRUSHED through the thick buttercups at the road edge and said nothing.

…

The Kelveys came nearer, and beside them walked their shadows, very long, stretching right across the road with their heads in the buttercups.
The Doll's House

MARIGOLD *Calendula officinalis*

DAZZLING WHITE the picotees shone; the golden-eyed marigolds glittered …
At the Bay (VI)

I HAVE JUST EATEN a juicy, meaty orange … And they're not only food for the body – they positively *flash* in my room, a pyramid of them, with, on either side, attending, a jar of the brightest, biggest, vividest marigolds I've ever seen.
Letter to JMM, Cornwall, 6 June 1918

WHAT AN AWFUL PULL you have over us aged flowers at being such a little short of spring yourself. You're no older than a jonquil for all your big overcoats & I'm a kind of late – late – let's see – I'll say marigold because I love them.
Letter to Richard Murry, Isola Bella, late November 1920

IT'S STRANGE we should all of us Beauchamps have this passion for flowers … I have a large bunch of the good old-fashioned marigolds on my table, buds, leaves and all. *They* take me back to that black vase of ours at 75 [Tinakori Rd], one that you used to like to put mignonette in.
Letter to her sisters Charlotte and Jeanne, Paris, 1 March 1922

THE MARYGOLDS unclosèd are.
Letter to JMM, Ospedaletti, Italy, 15 October 1919 (an allusion to a romantic ballad)

KM wearing a daisy (or possibly a marigold).
Alexander Turnbull Library MNZ-2532-1/2-F

I WISH YOU could see the marigolds on our table. They are like little stars in their own firmament – Jack bought them. They are good flowers to buy. Remember them when you set up house. They last well and are always so full of life. There is also, little painter brother, a fine sky this afternoon – big rolling clouds. In fact it's spring here …
Letter to Richard Murry, Paris, 3 March 1922

ANEMONE *Anemone coronaria*

EVERYWHERE there are clusters of china blue pansies, a mist of forget-me-nots, a tangle of anemones. Strange that these anemones – scarlet and amethyst and purple – vibrant with colour, always appear to me a trifle dangerous, sinister, seductive but poisonous.
In the Botanical Gardens, Unbound papers, 1907

I HAVE BEEN WANTING to write to you for nearly three weeks – I *have* been writing to you ever since Murry came and said: 'there's a perfectly wonderful woman in England' and told me about you. Since then I have wanted to send you things, too – some anemones, purple and crimson lake and a rich, lovely white, some blue irises that I found growing in the grass, too frail to gather, certain places in the woods where I imagine you would like to be – and certain hours like this hour of bright moonlight, when the flowering almond tree hangs over our white stone verandah a blue shadow with long tassels.
Letter to Ottoline Morrell, Bandol, 21 January 1916

BUT WE WERE A FUNNY PARTY. Brett, like some delightful bird who had flown in, laughing through the bright anemone flowers.
Letter to Ottoline Morrell, London, 12 May 1918. Dorothy Brett was a witness when KM & JMM married on 3 May 1918.

JACK – YOU NEVER BOUGHT THEM. Such flowers are never seen except by lovers, and then – rarely – rarely. I have put all in the big jar & they are on the table before the mirror. You will never never know what joy they have given me – What is the good of sitting here at my writing table. All my little thoughts are turned into bees & butterflies & tiny humming-birds and are flown off. Now & again I take up the lamp & follow them –

Were they like this when you bought them? Or did the lovely act of your buying them cause them to put on this beautiful attire – Oh me, I don't know!

But please remember that when my heart is opened, there will be: item, one bouquet of Anemones presented by her true love, March 7th 1919.

Thank you for Ever More.
Letter to JMM, Hampstead, 7 March 1919

HERE – AFTER THE JOURNEY – was this room waiting for me – exquisite – large with four windows overlooking great gardens & mountains – wonderful flowers … I have a big writing table with a cut glass inkstand – a waste paper basket – a great bowl of violets and *your* own anemones & wallflowers in it.
Letter to JMM, L'Hermitage, Menton, 21 January 1920

BY THE WAY do coloured anemones do well with you? One never seems to see them in English gardens and they are so decorative and last so well when they are cut. I have beauties in my room now and they are a week old. I should think they'd grow well in your climate – where it's warm and sheltered.
Letter to her sister Charlotte, Paris, 26 March 1922

> **But please remember that when my heart is opened, there will be: item, one bouquet of Anemones presented by her true love, March 7th 1919.**

ROSE *Rosa*

AS FOR THE ROSES, you could not help feeling they understood that roses are the only flowers that impress people at garden-parties; the only flowers that everybody is certain of knowing.
The Garden Party

RED as the wine of forgotten ages
Yellow as gold by the sunbeams spun
Pink as the gowns of Aurora's pages
White as the robes of a sinless one
Sweeter than Araby's winds that blow
Roses. Roses I love you so.
Red as the wine of forgotten ages (1908)

THE ROSES were in flower – gentlemen's button-hole roses, little white ones, but far too full of insects to hold under anyone's nose, pink monthly roses with a ring of fallen petals round the bushes, cabbage roses on thick stalks, moss roses, always in bud, pink smooth beauties opening curl on curl, red ones so dark they seemed to turn black as they fell, and a certain exquisite cream kind with a slender red stem and bright scarlet leaves.
Prelude, VI

I THINK, BELOVED, that were we two together in the most deserted – god forsaken desert it would surely blossom as a rose – – I never knew before what Passion meant – this complete absorption of the one into the other …
Letter to Garnet Trowell, London, 7 October 1908

OH, TO SEE THE PERFECTION of the perfumed petals being changed ever so slightly, as though a thin flame had kissed each with hot breath, and where the wounds bled the colour is savagely intense … I have before me such a Rose, in a thin, clear glass, and behind it a little spray of scarlet leaves. Yesterday it was beautiful with a certain serene, tearful, virginal beauty; it was strong and wholesome, and the scent was fresh and invigorating. …
Study: The Death of a Rose, published in the Triad, 1908

BUT THE WALLPAPER hurt me physically. It hung in tattered strips from the wall. In its less discoloured and faded patches I could trace the pattern of roses – buds and flowers – and the frieze was a conventional design of birds, of what genus the good God alone knows. … The light filled the room with darkness. Like a sleepy child she slipped out of her frock, and then, suddenly, turned to me and flung her arms round my neck. Lo every bird upon the bulging frieze broke into song. Lo every rose upon the tattered paper budded and formed into blossom. Yes, even the green vine upon the bed curtains wreathed itself into strange chaplets and garlands, twined round us in a leafy embrace, held us with a thousand clinging tendrils.
    And Youth was not dead.
Leves Amores

MY ROSES ARE TOO LOVELY. They melt in the air … I have 23… they are very lovely, the dark red stems and a leaf or two showing through the water.
Letter to JMM, Bandol, France, 29 December 1915

THE WHOLE VILLAGE is adorned with roses, trees of roses, fields, hedges, they tumble over the steps in a shower, children wear them, hideous middleclass women in chocolate brown costumes with black button boots & hard velvet toques pull & twist them from the stems. I walk about wishing I knew the name of that white beauty with petals stained as though with wine and long slender buds – those pink ones round and curled – those red ones with *silver shadows.*
Letter to JMM, Ospedaletti, Italy, 23 November 1919

DID YOU EVER explore the village, darling? It is so lovely … it feels gay – rather fantastic. The air smelled of pines and of deep yellow roses which grow everywhere like weeds: they even climb up the aloe trees.
Letter to JMM, Ospedaletti, Italy, 13 November 1919

IT IS RAINING, a heavy misty rain – most beautiful … it was thrilling to hear the fine rain sting the stretched silk of my umbrella, the sudden heavy drops drum on it from the gum trees. All the coast is soft, soft colour, the roses hang heavy – the spiders' webs are hung with family jewels.
Letter to JMM, Ospedaletti, Italy, 25 November 1919

I WISH YOU COULD see my roses. They are so exquisite that yesterday I made Jones [Ida Baker] photograph them so that I should be able to show you how they looked.
Letter to Violet Schiff, Hampstead, 16 July 1920

IT'S SIMPLY HEAVENLY here today – warm, still, with wisps of cloud just here & there & le ciel [the sky] deep blue. Everything is expanding & growing after the rain; the buds on the tea roses are so exquisite that one feels quite faint regarding them. A pink rose – 'chinesy pink' in my mind – is out – there are multitudes of flowers and buds. And the freesias are up & the tangerines are turning.
Letter to JMM, Isola Bella, Menton, 1 November 1920

Katherine Mansfield and John Middleton Murry at the Villa Isola Bella, Menton, France.
Alexander Turnbull Library, 1/2-011908-F

THE TEA ROSES are in flower. Do you know the peculiar exquisite scent of a tea rose? Do you know how the bud opens – so unlike other roses and how deep red the thorns are and almost purple the leaves?
Letter to JMM, Isola Bella, Menton, 10 November 1920

I LOVE HEARING about your work: you must know I do always … I must get up & take the earwigs out of the roses. Why should they choose roses? But they do & I go against Nature in casting them forth.
Letter to Richard Murry, Isola Bella, Menton, 15 November 1920

IT'S A LOVELY DAY – but by the time you come all the leaves will be gone. The last are falling. I don't know about mes roses; at present the whole garden is roses – where it's not violets. The different smells of different roses – I've only this year realised. There are 6 in my garden. I go from one to the other until I feel like a bee.
Letter to JMM, Isola Bella, Menton, 3 December 1920

AS TO THAT WHITE ROSE bush over the gate & the gas meter it is sprinkled with thousands of tiny satin-fine clusters.
Letter to Ida Baker, Isola Bella, Menton, 8 March 1921

[My cousin] ELIZABETH WAS HERE yesterday and we lay in my room talking about flowers until we were really quite drunk – or I was. She – describing – 'a certain very exquisite *rose*, single, pale yellow with coral tipped petals' and so on. I kept thinking of little curly blue hyacinths and *white* violets and the bird cherry. My trouble is I had so many flowers when I was little, I got to know them so well that they are simply the breath of life to me. It's no ordinary love; it's a passion.
Letter to Dorothy Brett, Chalet des Sapins, Montana-sur-Sierre, Switzerland, 26 January 1922

Dorothy Brett, KM and Ida Baker in the garden at Sierre, Switzerland, 1921.
Alexander Turnbull Library 1/2-011925-F

II

Earliest memories

1888–1898

In 1893, when KM was four and a half, the Beauchamps — Harold and Annie, with their little girls, Vera, Charlotte ('Chaddie'), Kathleen ('Kass') and Jeanne, aged 12 months — moved from 11 (now 25) Tinakori Road, Thorndon, to semi-rural Karori, about four miles from the centre of Wellington. The extended family also included KM's dearly loved grandmother, with whom she shared a bed, and Annie's unmarried sister, Belle. 'Chesney Wold' in Karori, described in *Prelude*, had an orchard and a rambling garden full of both wild and cultivated flowers — including the thorny 'aloe'.

The Beauchamps' longed-for son Leslie was born in 1894. In *At the Bay* KM recalled a beach holiday when the baby ('the boy') lay beside his mother in the garden, beneath a flowering manuka. Just over the fence were the sand hills threaded with pink convolvulus, and then the sea.

Disliking her big sister Vera's bossy ways, and unable to play with Jeanne, who was still a toddler, Kass became the odd one out and often played alone. Through the voice of Kezia (pronounced to rhyme with desire, says her biographer, Antony Alpers) KM wrote about imaginative games she played with flowers, sometimes pretending they were shopkeepers: she could buy pepper in pepper pots at Mr Poppy's; eggs, ready poached, at Mr Daisy's… While at Queen's College, London, she wrote *My Potplants*, a fantasy about an orphan for whom flowers were 'her only companions':

> I thought of the time when I was quite a child and lived in the queer old rambling house … During my childhood I lived surrounded by a luxurious quantity of flowers, and they were my only companions … How I loved my life. My greatest delight then was to find fresh flowers to love, and my greatest sorrow if they should die. I remember the year when Spring was very late in coming. I had stolen out in the garden in the dead of night to cover with a blanket the little snowdrop I had found the day before.

ARUM LILY *Zantedeschia aethiopica*

THE DINING-ROOM window had a square of coloured glass at each corner. One was blue and one was yellow. Kezia bent down to have one more look at a blue lawn with blue arum lilies growing at the gate, and then at a yellow lawn with yellow lilies and a yellow fence.
Prelude, II

THE ROOM SMELT of lilies; there were two big jars of arums in the fire-place.
Prelude, XI

SHE BENT her face over the spicy arum lilies and could not have enough of their scent. 'I shall *remember* just this moment,' decided the little girl. 'I shall always remember what I like and forget what I don't like.' How still and quiet it was. She could hear the dew dripping off the leaves.
Kezia and Tui

IT WAS SPRING – our garden was full of big white lilies. I used to run out & sniff them & come in again with my nose all yellow.
A Recollection of Childhood

I WATCH the long succession of brown paddocks – beautiful with here, a thick spreading of buttercups – there a white sweetness of arum lilies ...
Urewera Notebook (Upper Hutt)

WILL YOU PLEASE guarder these snaps for me in a book? Don't forget mignonette, because I'll weep over the steps & the arum lilies – in memory.
    Do you think they are good of your girl? Please tell.
Letter to JMM, Villa Flora, Menton, 26 April 1920
('guarder these snaps': look after these photos)

CHERRY BLOSSOM *Prunus avium*

UNDERNEATH the cherry trees
The Grandmother in her lilac printed gown
Carried Little Brother in her arms.
A wind, no older than Little Brother,
Shook the branches of the cherry trees
So that the blossom snowed on her hair
And on her faded lilac gown
And all over Little Brother.
I said 'may I see?'
She bent down and lifted a corner of his shawl.
He was fast asleep.
But his mouth moved as if he were kissing.
'Beautiful,' said the Grandmother, nodding and smiling.
But my lips quivered,
And looking at her kind face
I wanted to be in the place of Little Brother
To put my arms round her neck
And kiss the two tears that shone in her eyes.
The Grandmother

POPPY *Papaver rhoeas*

SHE TURNED over to the wall and idly, with one finger, she traced a poppy on the wall-paper with a leaf and a stem and a fat bursting bud. In the quiet, and under her tracing finger, the poppy seemed to come alive. She could feel the sticky, silky petals, the stem, hairy like a gooseberry skin, the rough leaf and the tight glazed bud. Things had a habit of coming alive like that.
Prelude, v

PANSY *Viola tricolor var. hortensis*
VIRGINIA STOCK *Malcolmia maritima*

'AREN'T THE PANSIES pretties, Grannie? I'd like to make pets of them.'
 'I think they're rather like my little scaramouch in the face,' said Mrs Fairfield, smiling and pulling Kezia's pink ear.
Kezia and Tui

… THE SOFT MUSKY perfume of the little white pansies that spread down the garden like moths …
Notebook 8 (Notebooks, Volume One)

THERE UNDER a new-leafed tree, hung with little bunches of white flowers, she sat down on a green bench and looked over the Convent flower-beds. In the one nearest to her there grew tender stocks, with a border of blue, shell-like pansies …
Taking the Veil

LIKE COUNTRY CHILDREN in starched pinafores, soberly and a little tearfully gathered together at Sunday school, the pansies star my garden walks.
(Parody) for editor of New Age, 25 May 1911

AND PANSIES – little darlings they are! People don't pay half enough attention to pansies.…
It was the late afternoon

so she played there ever so many games. One nice one was 'paying calls'. She … visited all the houses in Box Hedge Street. There was the Pansy School where dear children with clean faces sang 'Gentle Jesus' and other songs that she taught them very carefully – the long words slowly – the Violet Family, who played 'Hide & Seek' all the day long, the rich 'Lady Hollyhock' and Sweet William – a *little* common – she had heard him say ''andsome' – but still very friendly.
The Thoughtful Child

COSMOS *Cosmos bipinnatus*

'have you seen my cosmias dear? Have you noticed my cosmias today? Really, even though they are mine I must say I've never seen so fine a show. Everybody remarks on them. People stop to stare. I think it's so marvellous of the children not to pick them now that they show over the fence.

'Those mauve ones. Did you ever see anything so delicate! Such an uncommon colour, too. And when I think all that beauty came out of one little 3d packet from the D.I.C!'

Frail as butterflies the petals of the cosmias fluttered like wings in the gently breathing air. They were moon white, mauve, pale pink, and lemon yellow. And peering through the delicate green you could still see in the garden bed, the little soiled seed packet stuck in a cleft stick. Kezia remembered the day when she had watched Aunt Fan tear off a corner, shake the seed, like minute canary seed, then pat the fine earth over. […] Kezia smiled at an exquisite half-open bud, the petals springing from the centre like the feathers of a tiny shuttlecock.

Have you seen my cosmias, dear?

CAMELLIA
Camellia japonica

THEY WERE STANDING by the red and white camellia trees. Beautiful were the rich dark leaves spangled with light and the round flowers that perch among them like red and white birds.
Prelude, XI

THE CAMELLIAS were in bloom, white and crimson and pink and white striped with flashing leaves.
Prelude, VI

DARK DARK the leaves of the camellia tree
The flowers of the camellia tree
Are whiter far than snow.
I could drown myself in you
Lose myself in your embrace.
Song of the Camellia Blossoms

SWEET WILLIAM *Dianthus barbatus*

SHE SAT AT THE TABLE her hands just touching the long paper of mixed flowers that the landlady had given her to take home. They *were* mixed. Canterbury bells, sweet william like velvet pincushions, irises, silly flaring poppies, snapdragon and some roses that smell sweetly in water lay half spoiled with greenfly.
The Boy with the Jackdaw (The Quarrel)

I CAME HOME to find another huge bouquet from his garden – mixed sweet williams – superb great velvet flowers – white & pink and red. My room looks *full* of them …
Letter to JMM, Cornwall, 16 June 1918

PICOTEE *Dianthus caryophyllus*

DAZZLING WHITE the picotees shone …
At the Bay (VI)

UP A LITTLE PATH of round white pebbles they went, with drenched sleeping flowers on either side. Grandma's delicate white picotees were so heavy with dew that they were fallen, but their sweet smell was part of the cold morning.
The Voyage

RED HOT POKER *Kniphofia*
JAPANESE WINDFLOWER* *Anemone hupehensis*

THE RED-HOT pokers were taller than she; the Japanese sunflowers grew in a tiny jungle. She sat down on one of the box borders. By pressing hard at first it made a nice seat. But how dusty it was inside! Kezia bent down to look and sneezed and rubbed her nose.
Prelude, VI

* Japanese windflowers, not Japanese sunflowers, match this description.

FUCHSIA *Fuchsia magellanica*

DRENCHED were the cold fuchsias …
At the Bay (I)

THE FUCHSIA BUSH was tall. It fell over the fence in a shower. There was a little pit of darkness beneath.
At the Bay (XII)

SEA CONVOLVULUS *Calystegia soldanella*

THE SUN BEAT DOWN, beat down hot and fiery on the fine sand, baking the grey and blue and black and white-veined pebbles. It sucked up the little drop of water that lay in the hollow of the curved shells; it bleached the pink convolvulus that threaded through and through the sand-hills.
At the Bay (VII)

I MUST STOP this letter & get on with my new story. It's called At the Bay & it's (I hope) full of sand and seaweed and bathing dresses hanging over verandahs & sandshoes on window sills, and little pink 'sea' convolvulus, and rather gritty sandwiches and the tide coming in. And it smells (oh I DO hope it smells) a little bit fishy.
Letter to Dorothy Brett, Chalet des Sapins, Switzerland, 4 August 1921

NASTURTIUM *Tropaeolum majus*

… ROUND PEARLS of dew lay on the flat nasturtium leaves.
At the Bay (I)

… THE NASTURTIUMS wreathed the veranda poles in green and gold flame. If only one had time to look at these flowers long enough, time to get over the sense of novelty and strangeness, time to know them! But as soon as one paused to part the petals, to discover the under-side of the leaf, along came Life and one was swept away.
At the Bay (VI)

MORE BEAUTIFUL by far than a
morning in Spring or Summer.
The mist – the trees
standing in it – not a
leaf moves – not a
breath stirs […] The
nasturtiums blaze in
the garden; their
leaves are pale.
*Notebook 25
(Notebooks, Volume
Two), 12 July 1920*

ALL HER CHILDHOOD
had been passed in a long white
house perched on a hill overlooking
Wellington harbour – a house with a wild garden
full of bushes and fruit-trees, long, thick grass and nasturtiums. Nasturtiums
grew everywhere – there was no fighting them down. They even fell in
a shower over the paling fence on to the road. Red, yellow, white, every
possible colour; they lighted the garden like swarms of butterflies.
The Aloe

VERBENA *Verbena x hybrida*

'DO YOU REMEMBER that first afternoon we
spent together at Kew Gardens? You were
so surprised because I did not know the
names of any flowers. I am still just as
ignorant for all your telling me. But
whenever it is very fine and warm, and
I see some bright colours – it's awfully
strange – I hear your voice saying:
"Geranium, marigold, and verbena."
And I feel those three words are all I
recall of some forgotten, heavenly
language … You remember that
afternoon? …

Yes, it had been a wonderful afternoon, full of geranium and marigold and verbena, and – warm sunshine. Her thoughts lingered over the last two words as though she sang them.
A Dill Pickle

LEMON VERBENA
Aloysia citrodora

LINDA PULLED a piece of verbena and crumpled it, and held her hands to her mother.

'Delicious,' said the old woman.
Prelude, XI

YOUR WONDERFUL LETTER which seemed with its spray of verbena to come flying through the gold and green September air dropped in my lap and I read it and sniffed and sniffed the sweet spray and put it at the bottom of a blue jar.
Letter to Ottoline Morrell, London, 23 September 1917

HOW AM I to thank you for your letter and for these exquisite flowers? They are both so perfect – they are like *one* gift – and it's strangely true – how just as your letters *are* you – so the flowers you send couldn't have been sent by anybody else – I feel I could single out this bright sweet bouquet in Eternity & say – they came from Ottoline. You have such a lovely way of gathering flowers as you talk – or of suddenly handing one a piece of verbena or scented geranium – almost, as it were, unconsciously –
Letter to Ottoline Morrell, London, 15 August 1918

HOW LOVELY Garsington must be! The grass, the shadows of the trees, the lemon verbena in the flower garden. I can see it all.
Letter to Ottoline Morrell, Switzerland, late May 1921

AGAVE *Agave americana*

KM is describing the American agave, not an aloe.

NOTHING GREW on the top except one huge plant with thick, grey-green, thorny leaves, and out of the middle there sprang up a tall stout stem. Some of the leaves of the plant were so old that they curled up in the air no longer; they turned back, they were split and broken; some of them lay flat and withered on the ground.

Whatever could it be? She had never seen anything like it before. She stood and stared. And then she saw her mother coming down the path.

'Mother, what is it?' asked Kezia.

Linda looked up at the fat swelling plant with its cruel leaves and fleshy stem. High above them, as though becalmed in the air, and yet holding so fast to the earth it grew from, it might have had claws instead of roots. The curving leaves seemed to be hiding something; the blind stem cut into the air as if no wind could ever shake it.

'That is an aloe, Kezia,' said her mother.

'Does it ever have any flowers?'

'Yes, Kezia,' and Linda smiled down at her, and half shut her eyes. 'Once every hundred years.'

Prelude, VI

'I LIKE THAT ALOE. I like it more than anything here. And I am sure I shall remember it long after I've forgotten all the other things.'

… Looking at it from below she could see the long sharp thorns that edged the aloe leaves, and at the sight of them her heart grew hard … She particularly liked the long sharp thorns.

Prelude, XI

out of the middle there sprang up a tall stout stem

III

Ablaze in Wellington gardens

1898–1903

When KM was ten — the year she first read *Elizabeth and her German Garden*, written by her father's first cousin who had married a German count — the family moved from Karori back into town. At first they lived in the large house at 75 Tinakori Road, with lavender, roses and lilies in the garden. (This was where 'the Sheridans' held their famous *Garden Party*; in her 'Laura Sheridan' stories KM recalled some of her experiences as a girl in Thorndon, Wellington.)

With her elder sisters Vera and Charlotte, Kass walked to Wellington Girls' College, and later to Miss Mary Swainson's select private school where her untidy work and her ideas were criticised and unappreciated, and a foolish comment was written: 'She put *herself* in too much'. KM's mocking revenge was to 'borrow' the name of her dignified headmistress for a character in *The Wind Blows* — the fictional Marie Swainson was totally *un*dignified, stamping her foot and swearing as the wind blew her skirt over her head.

KM went to her music lessons on foot, carrying her cello. She fell in love with her music teacher's son Tom (Arnold) Trowell, a talented cellist (and, later, with his twin brother Garnet, who played the violin). She wandered into the nearby convent garden in Hill Street with its beds of freesias and pansies, and explored the Botanic Garden with its dramatic rhododendrons, magnolias and cabbage trees. Wherever she walked, KM looked 'over the low painted fences' and observed well-tended flower gardens.

KARAKA *Corynocarpus laevigatus*

THEN THE KARAKA-TREES would be hidden. And they were so lovely, with their broad, gleaming leaves, and their clusters of yellow fruit. They were like trees you imagined growing on a desert island, proud, solitary, lifting their leaves and fruits to the sun in a kind of silent splendour. Must they be hidden by a marquee?

The Garden Party

LAVENDER *Lavandula spica*

HE BENT DOWN, pinched a sprig of lavender, put his thumb and forefinger to his nose and snuffed up the smell. When Laura saw the gesture she forgot all about the karakas in her wonder at him caring for things like that – caring for the smell of lavender. How many men that she knew would have done such a thing.

The Garden Party

JUST UNDER HER WINDOW a boy was singing:

'Ladies fair, I bring to you
Sweet lavender with spikes of blue.'

in a fresh, rough, vigorous voice. His basket was full of little bunches of the fragrant dainty blossom. Audrey felt she would like to buy it all, crush it in her hands, bury her face in it, absorb it.

The Education of Audrey

[…] HAD A TALK to their jardinier who comes here le vendredi to plant flowers autour de la palmier [around the palm tree]. This man drew a design of the flower bed on the gravel, & then after telling me the names of the flowers he described them. You know Bogey it was *terrific* to hear him. In trying to describe the scent – c'est–un–parrr-fum – & then he threw back his head put his thumb & forefinger to his nose – took a *long* breath &

suddenly exploded it in a kind of AAAHHH, almost
staggering backwards – overcome – almost fainting …
I sat down on a bench & felt as though waves of health
went flowing through me. To think the man *cares*
like that – *responds* – laughs like he does and
snips off a rosebud for you while he talks.
Letter to JMM, Isola Bella, Menton, 13 October 1920

YOUR MENTIONING the verbena made me think of
the lavender bushes last year – and the morning we
sat in the garden for a little while. I always see *across*
our conversation those lovely spikes of deep purplish
blue, and the bees were busy in them. That and the
sound of water and the flight of three swallows – all are
'important' to the moment.
Letter to Sydney Schiff, Isola Bella, Menton, 3 November 1920

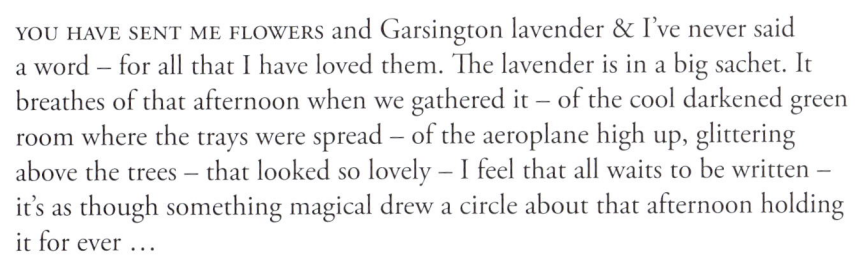

YOU HAVE SENT ME FLOWERS and Garsington lavender & I've never said
a word – for all that I have loved them. The lavender is in a big sachet. It
breathes of that afternoon when we gathered it – of the cool darkened green
room where the trays were spread – of the aeroplane high up, glittering
above the trees – that looked so lovely – I feel that all waits to be written –
it's as though something magical drew a circle about that afternoon holding
it for ever …
Letter to Ottoline Morrell, Hampstead, 13 August 1919

In her memoir *Ottoline at Garsington: Memoirs of Lady Ottoline Morrell, 1915-1918*, she recalled collecting lavender with Mansfield to make potpourri: 'The lavender was ripe for cutting and Katherine and I with knives and scissors cut and cut and made great piles of it, laying it out on a sheet to dry. How we both loved that strong aromatic smell which would permeate the house when it was brought in. Then she would linger round me when I was collecting the herbs, sweet geranium and verbena, the rose leaves and rosemary for *pot-pourri*. She would wander about and come back with a handful of green herbs to throw into my basket. She really loved the garden …'

they are like white shells
Afloat on the crest
of a sea wave

PASSION VINE *Passiflora caerulea*

SHE SAT ON THE BROAD window-sill, her hands clasped loosely in her lap. Just below her in the garden a passion flower twined round a little fence – in the half-light the blossoms were like pale hands among the leaves. In the distance a little belt of pine trees, dark & motionless against a saffron evening sky.
Notebook 1 (Notebooks, Volume One), 1907

A passion vine twists over the fence,
Like white birds the blossoms among the leaves

O, no, they are like white shells
Afloat on the crest of a sea wave.

The passion vine trembles as though it will break
Just like a wave – spilling its shining treasure
Over the desolate shores of my darkened garden.

… A passion vine twists over the fence
Like faint thoughts the blossoms among the leaves.

O, yes, they are like faint thoughts
Afloat on the crest of my sorrow.

The passion vine trembles as though it will break
Just like my sorrow – spilling its fainting treasure
Over the desolate shores of my darkened heart.
Thought Dreams

ORANGE-BALL TREE* *Buddleja globosa*

AND MRS SHERIDAN woke out of her dream to find herself standing under a beautiful mock orange bush that grew against the white palings of old Mr Phipps' garden. The little sponge-like fruit – flowers? which were they? – shone burning-bright in the late afternoon sun. They are like little worlds, she thought, peering up through the large crumpled leaves and she put out her hand and touched one gently. The feel of things is so strange, so different: one never seems to know a thing until one has felt it – at least that is true of flowers. Roses for instance – who can smell a rose without kissing it …

Now her glove was all brushed with yellow. But it didn't matter. She was glad, even. 'I wish you grew in my garden,' she said regretfully to the mock orange bush, and she went on, thinking I wonder why I love flowers so much. None of the children inherit it from me – Laura, perhaps. But even then it's not the same – she's too young to feel as I do. I love flowers more than people – except my own family of course.

It was the late afternoon
*The orange-ball tree, not the mock-orange, matches this description.

WALLFLOWER *Erysimum cheiri*

THAT HEAVY EVENING RAIN that made waterspouts of Jack's trousers fell like a blessing upon the garden. When I went out today the air smelt like moss, and there was a bee to every wallflower.

Letter to Ida Baker, Isola Bella, Menton, 8 March 1921

MIRIAM COULD REMAIN indoors no longer. … The trees waved to her, she smelt the wild sweetness of the wallflower growing by the gate … I'll pick a big bunch and take them with me, she said, nodding gravely. … She stepped out of the house quickly, down the

narrow path to the wallflowers. So strong the scent it almost seemed to drag her into it. She knelt down on the grass border and cut a great spray of them …
Notebook 8 (Notebooks, Volume One)

AND JULIETTE has filled my vases with yellow goldy wallflowers – God! how I love flowers …
Letter to JMM, Bandol, France, 23 February 1918

MAGNOLIA *Magnolia x soulangeana*

THE BIG DARK HOUSE hid secretly
Behind the magnolia and the spreading pear-tree
But there was a sound of music – music rippled and ran
Like a lady laughing behind her fan
Laughing and mocking and running away –
Come into the garden – it's as light as day!
Night-Scented Stock

… AND THE PEARL ROSE loving-cup of a magnolia hangs delicately on the grey bough.
In the Botanical Gardens

THE GREAT RAIN has brought a thousand green spears up in every corner of the garden. Oh, you'll be met by such Flowers on Parade at Christmas Time … the magnolia flashes leaves; it has great buds brushed over with pink.
Letter to JMM, Isola Bella, Menton, 25 September 1920

OH SUN – shine forever! I feel a little bit drunk – rather like an insect that has fallen into the cup of a magnolia.
Letter to Dorothy Brett, Hampstead, 18 July 1919

hyacinths, so pink and white,
the colour of coconut ice

HYACINTH *Hyacinthus orientalis*

OVER THE LOW PAINTED fences, you could see, as you ran by, whose daffys were out, whose wild snowdrop border was over and who had the biggest hyacinths, so pink and white, the colour of coconut ice.
Weak Heart

Viola ran over to the table and put her arms round the jar of hyacinths.
'Beautiful! Beautiful!' she cried, burying her head in the flowers and sniffing greedily at the scent.
from The Swing of the Pendulum (In a German Pension)

CANNA LILY *Canna*

THERE, JUST INSIDE the door, stood a wide, shallow tray full of pots of pink lilies. No other kind. Nothing but lilies – canna lilies, big pink flowers, wide open, radiant, almost frighteningly alive on bright crimson stems.

'O-oh, Sadie!' said Laura, and the sound was like a little moan. She crouched down as if to warm herself at that blaze of lilies; she felt they were in her fingers, on her lips, growing in her breast.
The Garden Party

'WHAT DID I SAY?' shouted the Herr Professor under cover of tumultuous applause, 'tem-per-ament! There you have it. She is a flame in the heart of a lily.'
The Modern Soul

HYDRANGEA *Hydrangea macrophylla*

AND THEN HE FACED the big white-painted house, with its wide-open windows … its blue jars of hyacinths on the broad sills. On either side of the carriage porch their hydrangeas – famous in the town – were coming into flower; the pinkish, bluish masses of flower lay like light among the spreading leaves. And somehow, it seemed to old Mr Neave that the house and the flowers, and even the fresh marks on the drive, were saying, 'There is young life here …'
An Ideal Family

I AM IN THE MIDDLE of a new long story called Family Life which may surprise people a bit. I try & make Family Life so gorgeous – not hatred and cold linoleum – but warmth & hydrangeas –
Letter to Anne Rice, Isola Bella, Menton, January 1921

RHODODENDRON *Rhododendron*

BEFORE ME two great rhododendron bushes. Against the dark, broad leaves the blossoms rise, flame-like, tremulous in the still air …
In the Botanical Gardens

I LOOK OUT through the window … The sun shines whitely, touches the rhododendron leaves with soft colour. To and fro the branches sway, stretching upwards, outwards, so mysteriously; it is as though they moved in a dream.
Vignette: 'I look out through the window', 1908, Notebooks, Volume One

DAFFODIL *Narcissus*

A SUNLIT WONDER of chiming daffodils.
In the Botanical Gardens

LATE IN THE NIGHT – when I lie awake
Comes the quiet and secret moon to make
Delicate lamplight for my sake.

And from my window – down below
There is a box where the Spring flowers grow
Daffodils golden breathe and blow.
I am quite happy for you to see

ON MY TABLE are wild daffodils – Shakespeare daffodils. They are so lovely that each time I look up I give them to you again.
Letter to JMM, Bandol, France, 18 February 1918

JOHN BROUGHT ME A BUNCH of daffodils yesterday, the little half wild kind that smell sweet – far lovelier than the others, I always think. Garden daffodils are so plump and self-contained, rather like ducks.
Letter to 'Elizabeth' (Countess Russell), Paris, 6 March 1922

CHADDIE WROTE yesterday she had been gathering daffodils in the *fields* all the afternoon. It is a marvellous year for wild daffodils & pussy willows.
Letter to Ida Baker, Paris, 13 March 1922

FREESIA *Freesia*

THAT HEAVY evening rain … fell like a blessing upon the garden … The peach leaves are like linnet wings; the branches of the fig are touched with green, the bush of may is just not in flower. I had to lift up the daffodils & set them on their legs again and to give a finger to the reclining freezias. But nothing had come to harm.
Letter to Ida Baker, Isola Bella, Menton, 8 March 1921

… AT ONE CORNER a clump of creamy freezias, their light spears of green criss-crossed over the flowers.
Taking the Veil

BORONIA *Boronia megastigma*

CAN I BE OFFICIAL godmother to the garden? I should like to STARTLE you with the most superb things and to send for seeds from far corners of the earth and have a boronia plant below the studio window. Do you know the scent of boronia? My grandma and I were very fond of going to a place called McNabs Tea gardens and there we used to follow our noses and track down the boronia bushes. Oh how I must have tired the darling out! It doesn't bear thinking about.
Letter to Dorothy Brett, Paris, 14 February 1922

CINERARIA *Pericallis × hybrida*

OH, YOUR CINERARIAS. I wish I could see them. Do you know the blue ones, too? And the faint faint pink kind? Mother loved them. We used to grow masses in a raised flower bed. I loved the shape of the petals – it is so delicate. We used to have blue ones in pots in a rather white and gold drawing room that had green wooden sun blinds.
Letter to Dorothy Brett, Paris, 15 March 1922

… AS YOU CAN SEE I'm in France. It's lovely weather – warm – mild – the air smells of faint far off tangerines with just a touch of nutmeg. On my table there are cornflowers & jonquils with rosemary sprigs … The flowers are wonderful. How lovely the earth is. Do you know I had fifteen cinerarias in Italy & they grew against the sea? I hope one will be able to call these things up on one's deathbed.
Letter to Sylvia Lynd, L'Hermitage, Menton, 31 January 1920

FORGET-ME-NOT *Myosotis sylvatica*

WE DREW REIN – & there was a wide space of blue forget-me-nots …
Urewera Notebook (near the Aratiatia Rapids)

A MIST of forget-me-nots
In the Botanical Gardens

VIBURNUM (LAURUSTINUS)
Viburnum tinus

IT IS EVENING and very cold. From my window the laurestinus bush, in this half light looks weighted with snow. It moves languidly, gently, backwards and forwards, and each time I look at it a delicate flower melody fills my brain.
Silhouettes

… OPENING HER WINDOW, from the new-mown lawn
The fragrant, fragrant scent of perfumed grass
The lilac tossing in the shining air
Its purple plumes. The laurustinus bush
Its blossoms like pale hands among the leaves
Quivered and swayed …
The Winter Fire

CLEMATIS *Clematis lanuginosa*

HENRY SAT on the verandah edge, eating his orange and looking at the clematis flowers. Wide open, dazzling, they lay – as if waiting in rapture for the moon. It was strange how frightfully they added to his excitement. He began to quiver all over. He thought, absurdly:– 'The top of my head feels just like one of those flowers' …
To the Last Moment

A LITTLE PIANO stood against the wall with yellow pleated silk let into the carved front. Above it hung an oil painting by Beryl of a large cluster of surprised looking clematis. Each flower was the size of a small saucer, with a centre like an astonished eye fringed in black.
Prelude, XI

IV

The bright flowers of Europe

1903–1923

In 1903 Harold and Annie Beauchamp sent 15-year-old Kathleen and her two older sisters 'Home' to central London for their final three years of schooling. Annie's first cousin, a London doctor, suggested Queen's College in Harley Street, an avant-garde school with university-style lectures, where he sent his own daughters. KM's time at Queen's inspired several of her stories — *Carnation* recalled a French lecture on a hot afternoon, and the crushed character of Con in *The Daughters of the Late Colonel* was based on Ida Baker, a fellow pupil with a bullying father.

Apart from a reluctant 18-month interlude back in New Zealand, KM lived in Europe for the rest of her life, and set many stories there. *Bliss* described a London house where a 'perfect, slender pear tree' was in blossom, and in a notebook she joked about 'arrogant' red geraniums 'shouting' at her — a colonial intruder who didn't belong in Hampstead.

KM often travelled to the continent. In 1906 she paid her first visit to Paris, which she loved. She spent six traumatic months in Bavaria, Germany, in 1909 and later visited Belgium, Italy and Switzerland, where she wrote some of her finest stories. In every country she noticed the flowers, writing to Dorothy Brett from the Chalet des Sapins on 25 July 1921:

> We have a real peasant girl who looks after everything … She is made to be painted … When she comes back after her afternoon out with a great bouquet of flowers and stands at the door holding them I wish Van Gogh was still alive!

She went to the south of France several times to avoid English winters. In her voluminous letters to Murry she mentioned flowers that impressed her, such as horse chestnut and japonica, and wrote about planning their own dream garden, with peonies, in England. But because of lack of funds, ill-health and frequent moves, it never happened.

CARNATION *Dianthus caryophyllus*

ON THOSE HOT DAYS Eve – curious Eve – always carried a flower. She snuffed it and snuffed it, twirled it in her fingers, laid it against her cheek, held it to her lips, tickled Katie's neck with it, and ended, finally, by pulling it to pieces and eating it, petal by petal.

'Roses are delicious, my dear Katie,' she would say, standing in the dim cloak room, with a strange decoration of flowery hats on the pegs behind her – 'but carnations are simply divine! They taste like – like – ah well!' And away her little thin laugh flew, fluttering among those huge, strange flower heads on the wall behind her. (But how cruel her little thin laugh was! It had a long sharp beak and claws and two bead eyes, thought fanciful Katie.)

To-day it was a carnation. She brought a carnation to the French class, a deep, deep red one, that looked as though it had been dipped in wine and left in the dark to dry. She held it on the desk before her, half shut her eyes and smiled.

'Isn't it a darling!' said she …

… She made a warm, white cup of her fingers – the carnation inside. Oh, the scent! It floated across to Katie. It was too much. Katie turned away to the dazzling light outside the window.
Carnation

LAST NIGHT I dreamed we were together in the country – *happy*, my dear, laughing like children – and at this moment I see myself slipping a carnation into your coat for a buttonhole – I can smell that strange carnation perfume – mystic and passionately sweet.
Letter to Garnet Trowell, London, 7 October 1908

I WISH YOU were *here*. Dark England is so far and this room smells spicy and sweet from the carnations – pink and red and wonderful yellow … I shall come back to dark England soon …
Letter to Ottoline Morrell, Bandol, France, 22 February 1918

TULIP *Tulipa*

STRANGE FLOWER, half opened, scarlet
So soft to feel and press
My lips upon your petals
Inhaled restlessness

A fever and a longing
Desire that burns in me
A violent scarlet passion
Stirs me so savagely.

Strange flowers half opened, scarlet
Show me your heart of flame
Do you keep it in silken wrapping
I shall find it all the same
I shall kiss your scarlet petals
Till they open your heart for me
And a beautiful tremulous passion

Shall bind us, savagely.
Scarlet Tulips

IF SHE WANTED to buy flowers, the car pulled up at that perfect shop in Regent Street, and Rosemary inside the shop just gazed in her dazzled, rather exotic way, and said: 'I want those and those and those. Give me four bunches of those. And that jar of roses. Yes, I'll have all the roses in the jar. No, no lilac. I hate lilac. It's got no shape.' The attendant bowed and put the lilac out of sight, as though this was only too true; lilac was dreadfully shapeless. 'Give me those stumpy little tulips. Those red and white ones.' And she was followed to the car by a thin shop-girl staggering under an immense white paper armful that looked like a baby in long clothes …
A Cup of Tea

> We named the flowers she brought each week. I remember two glorious tulips, one a great rich brown satin fellow, the other a smart little scarlet bud, thin and perky – 'Dignity and Impudence'.
>
> — Millie Parker, quoted in *The Life of Katherine Mansfield* by Ruth Elvish Mantz & J Middleton Murry

DOWN BELOW, in the garden beds, the red and yellow tulips, heavy with flowers, seemed to lean upon the dusk. A grey cat, dragging its belly, crept across the lawn, and a black one, its shadow, trailed after.
Bliss

THE EXQUISITE TULIPS & some sprigs of rosemary & verbena have brought your flower garden into my room. How I love them! Each time I get up from the writing table I go over to them and take a long long look – And oh – I want to say to them: live for ever! Don't fade – don't die. If you knew how we have longed for you you would not have the heart to be one petal less perfect than you are – at any rate not for a long time – Thank you for them, dearest friend.
Letter to Ottoline Morrell, Hampstead, London, 23 May 1919

I HAVE BEEN COSSETING four yellow tulips all this last week and they are still radiant. Oh, how I love flowers! People always say it must be because I spent my childhood among all those gorgeous tropical trees and blossoms. But I don't seem to remember us making our daisy chains of magnolias – do you?
Letter to her sister Charlotte, Paris, 19 February 1922

GERANIUM *Pelargonium x hortorum*

THE RED GERANIUMS have bought the garden over my head. They are there, established, back in the old home, every leaf and flower unpacked and in its place – and quite determined that no power on earth will ever move them again … But why should they make me feel a stranger? Why should they ask me every time I go near: 'And what are *you* doing in a London garden?' They burn with arrogance & pride. And I am the little colonial walking in the London garden patch – allowed to look, perhaps, but not to linger. If I lie on the grass they positively shout at me. Look at her lying on *our* grass, pretending she lives here, pretending this is her garden … She is a stranger – an alien. She is nothing but a little girl sitting on the Tinakori hills & dreaming:

I went to London and married an englishman & we lived in a tall grave house with red geraniums & white daisies in the garden at the back. *Im*-pudence!
Notebook 16 (Notebooks, Volume Two), 21 May 1919

THERE WERE CLUMPS of fairy bells, and all kinds of geraniums, and there were little trees of verbena and bluish lavender bushes and a bed of pelargoniums with velvet eyes and leaves like moths' wings.
Prelude, VI

THREE SUPERB GERANIUMS still stand on the ledge when it's fine, and their rosy masses of flowers against *blue space* are wonderful. It is so high up here that one only sees the tops & halfway down of the enormous mountains opposite, and there's a great sweep of sky …
Letter to Dorothy Brett, Chalet des Sapins, Switzerland, 11 November 1921

BESIDE ME a little bowl of mignonette is piercingly sweet, and a cluster of scarlet geraniums is hot with colour.
Vignette

DAPHNE *Daphne odora*

I THINK I SHALL become a very violent gardener. I shall have shelves of tomes & walk about the house whispering the names of flowers. We must have a tiny potting shed, too, just big enough for you & me. I see as I write little small forked sticks with labels on them. Daphne grows in England: Eden Phillpotts has a great bush. I shall write for a cutting.
Letter to JMM, Villa Flora, Menton, 22 February 1920

IF I LIVE HERE much longer I shall become a bush of daphne or you'll find no one to welcome you but a jasmine. Perhaps it's the effect of receiving the Sun every morning – très intime – the lady clad only in a black paper fan. But you must come here, you must live here in the South and forget greyness. It is *divine* here – no less.
Letter to JMM, Isola Bella, Menton, 10 November 1920

PEONY *Paeonia officinalis*

DEAREST
The flowers! I came in from posting your book and the whole house had a sweet scent. What peonies! And the roses. I am saving the petals to dry.
Letter to Ottoline Morrell, London, 12 June 1919

THINK OF THE FIRST time we visit it together, sitting on a step with our hats on our knees smoking a cigarette (man with a vehicle waiting for us somewhere round a corner) looking over the garden, feeling the house behind us, saying – we must have peonies under these windows.
Letter to JMM, Ospedaletti, Italy, 26 November 1919

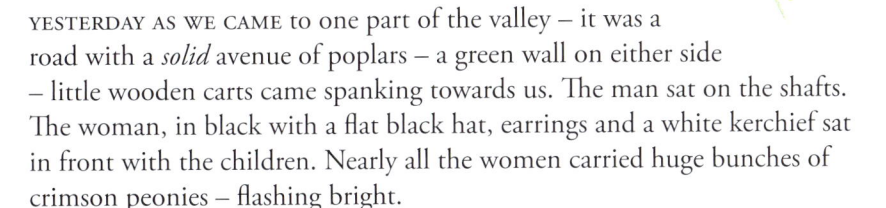

YESTERDAY AS WE CAME to one part of the valley – it was a road with a *solid* avenue of poplars – a green wall on either side – little wooden carts came spanking towards us. The man sat on the shafts. The woman, in black with a flat black hat, earrings and a white kerchief sat in front with the children. Nearly all the women carried huge bunches of crimson peonies – flashing bright.
Letter to JMM, Clarens-Montreux, Switzerland, 15 May 1921

I SHALL HAVE A GARDEN one day and work in it, too. Plant, weed, tie up, throw over the wall. And the peony border really will be staggering. Oh, how I love flowers! I think of them with such longing. I go through them, one after another, remembering them from their first moments with love – oh with rapture as if they were babies! No, it's what other women feel for babies – perhaps.
Letter to JMM, Paris, 13 October 1922

DOUBLE STOCK *Matthiola incana*

I HAVE REALLY loved her [my maid, Juliette] – and her songs, her ways … her rushes into the room with the big bouquets and her way of greeting one in the morning as though she loved the day … Goodbye Juliette, my charming double stock in flower.
*Letter to JMM, Bandol, France,
3 March 1918*

THE GARDEN IS FULL of double pink stocks. Gorgeous flowers, so strong and so sturdy. I wish I could send you an armful.
*Letter to Anne Drey, Isola Bella, Menton,
January 1921*

ON EITHER SIDE of the gravel are flower-beds full of purple and pink stocks, wallflowers, forget-me-nots and creamy freezias with their spears of tender green like the green of young bamboos. The front of the clinique is hung with heliotrope, banksia roses and pink ivy geranium. And there is such a coming and going of brown bees and white butterflies, the air smells so sweet, there is such a sense of delicate trembling life that, however ill anyone might be, it was impossible surely not to be cheered and distracted.
The Clinic Garden

GRAPE HYACINTH *Muscari armeniacum*

IT'S A PURE silver day. I have a blue & white glass of tiny blue hyacinths on my table. The day & the flowers say – Greece, to me & if I were a poet they would have a poem.
Letter to JMM, Isola Bella, Menton, 4 December 1920

PEAR *Pyrus communis*

THE WINDOWS of the drawing-room opened on to a balcony overlooking the garden. At the far end, against the wall, there was a tall, slender pear tree in fullest, richest bloom; it stood perfect, as though becalmed against the jade-green sky ... And she seemed to see on her eyelids the lovely pear tree with its wide open blossoms as a symbol of her own life. ...

And the two women stood side by side looking at the slender, flowering tree. Although it was so still it seemed, like the flame of a candle, to stretch up, to point, to quiver in the bright air, to grow taller and taller as they gazed – almost to touch the rim of the round, silver moon.

...

But the pear tree was as lovely as ever and as full of flower and as still.
Bliss

I WONDER if you feel too, this year more than any other year, a longing for the Spring to *stay* Spring. The flowers have fallen from the pear tree outside my window – just a few little silver petals are still spinning down – & the green is darker. I grudge it so. My Lotus Land would be an eternal first spring day when everything is in full leaf and the buds just unfolded.
Letter to Ottoline Morrell, Hampstead, 23 May 1919

I AM LOOKING for signs of spring already. Under the espalier pear trees there are wonderful Xmas roses [hellebore] which I saw for the first time this year. They reminded me of Switzerland, and somebody found four primroses the other day. I have moods when I simply pine for the S. of France or somewhere like Majorka [sic]. *When* this time is over I shall make for the South or the East & never go North again.
Letter to Ida Baker (not sent), Fontainebleau, Paris, early January 1923;
KM died on the evening of 9 January

I have 'planted out' some of my petunias into a story so that they may live a little longer

PETUNIA *Petunia x hybrida*

'WHAT ARE THOSE purple floppy flowers in my bedroom?' he murmured.
   'Petunias.'
   'You smell exactly like a petunia.'
   And he raised her up. She drew towards him. 'Kiss me,' said he.
All Serene!

… MY COUSIN ELIZABETH … was Von Arnheim – and now she's Countess Russell, Bertie's sister-in-law. Her love of flowers is really her greatest charm. Not that she says very much, but every word *tells*. A man wouldn't discover it in her – he wouldn't realise how deep it is. For no man loves flowers as women *can*. Elizabeth looks coolly at the exquisite petunias and says in a small faraway voice: 'They have a very perfect scent.' And I feel I can hear oceans of love breaking in her heart for petunias and nasturtiums and snapdragons. I believe you have been painting petunias – your purple velvety ones. Were they? Oh, we have the most wonderful ones here – SUCH colours. If I were an artist I could never resist them. But they must be difficult, because in spite of the weight of colour there's a transparent light shining through look in them. The look one imagines the fruits had in Aladdin's orchard …
Letter to Dorothy Brett, Chalet des Sapins, Montana-sur-Sierre, Switzerland, 4 August 1921

WE HAVE JUST been doing the flowers before we start work. Scene: the salle à manger, with windows wide open & pink curtings flapping. The table bare & heaped with petunias, snapdragons & nasturtiums. Glass vases & bowls full of water – a general sense of buds and wetness & that peculiar stickiness of fresh stalks. Jack – white shirt with sleeves up to his shoulders, white duck trousers & rope shoes snipping with a large pair of wet scissors. Me – blue cotton kimono & pink slippers afilling of the vases … Jack is *terribly* keen on petunias, I wish I could send you a whole great bastick full. They are

wonderful flowers – almost pure light – and yet an exquisite starry shape. We have every colour from pale pink to almost blackish purple. And do you know the smell of snapdragons?
Letter to Richard Murry, Chalet des Sapins, Montana-sur-Sierre, Switzerland, 9 August 1921

I FEEL I SHALL NEVER look at a bud or a flower again without thinking of you, and that there is an extra reason for saying – as one does – Praise Him – as one smells the petunias. I still 'in vacant or in pensive mood' go over those bunches you brought last summer – disentangle the sweet peas, marvel at the stickiness of the petunia leaves, come upon a sprig of very blithe carnations and shiver at the almost unearthly freshness of the nasturtiums.
Letter to Elizabeth, Countess Russell, Paris, 6 March 1922

I HAVE A WHOLE PETUNIA and nasturtium summer to thank you for – no less. Never shall I forget it. I know you will understand me when I say that every time I go into the salon they give me a fresh small shock of delight; every time one bends over them to greet them it is to discover fresh beauties. I have 'planted out' some of my petunias into a story so that they may live a little longer, and now I am looking for a favourable corner for a whole blaze of nasturtiums.
Letter to Elizabeth, Countess Russell, Chalet des Sapins, Montana-sur-Sierre, Switzerland, 22 August 1921

HOLLYHOCK *Alcea rosea*

IT HAD BEEN RAINING all the morning, late summer rain, warm, heavy, quick, and now the sky was clear, except for a long tail of little clouds, like ducklings, sailing over the forest. There was just enough wind to shake the last drops off the trees; one warm star splashed on his hand. Ping! – another drummed on his hat. The empty road gleamed, the hedges smelt of briar, and how big and bright the hollyhocks glowed in the cottage gardens.
Mr and Mrs Dove

LABURNUM *Laburnum anagyroides*

THE PARCEL arrived on Xmas morning … just your letter & the two enchanting sketches. I love them, Anne. They remind me of our spring together & the laburnum seems hung with little laughs.
Letter to Anne Rice, Isola Bella, Menton, 26 December 1920

SWEET PEA *Lathyrus odoratus*

THE GARDENER is here; he arrived at Aurora's heels, thumping his tail. I think he has done wonders but oh, I feel inclined to cry to the garden like I do to you when you've been to the barber: why did you let him take off *so much*. When will it grow again! My cotton plant has lost its curls, a ruthless chopping of them; the roses that had all started what I thought were the most exquisite promising shoots are cut down to the bone & told to try again. I must plant sweetpeas immediately. […] there on the path lie the pink geraniums – oh weh! oh weh! I feel there's an awful moral to be drawn out of all this & except ye can bear this to be done unto ye, ye shall not bring forth. At any rate some old gardener or other has been doing it to us for years: and God knows we've had our naked shivering moments – so now I shall *fill* this garden with flowers – I shall make it to blaze & shine & smell ravishing and look celestially beautiful by the time you come just to point the moral further.
Letter to JMM, Ospedaletti, Italy, 19 October 1919

TWO LADIES CAME on the front steps of the pension and stood, arm in arm, looking over the garden. The one, old and scraggy, dressed almost entirely in black bead trimming and a satin reticule; the other, young and thin, in a white gown, her yellow hair tastefully garnished with mauve sweet peas.
The Modern Soul

CROCUS *Crocus vernus*

YOUR CROCUS BORDER fills me with envy. How I love them!
Letter to her sisters Charlotte and Jeanne, Paris, 1 March 1922

I 'NOTE' ALSO that the rooks are building, the elm trees are in flower, there's a remarkable show of white crocuses in Kensington garden, the bird-cherry is out in the hedges, the fields are bright with coltsfoot, the male & female catkins are out, violets are in bloom, primroses, and bluebells are pushing up – All that was in the paper last week … the one good of newspapers is that kind of news.
Letter to Ida Baker, Paris, 13 March 1922

THE THOUGHTFUL CHILD knew 'most everything about Fairies. She had been one herself once, and lived in a crocus on the lawn. Oh, the dear house it made, and one day Father 'peeked' out of the window and saw the crocus and cut it with his penknife, and carried it ever so carefully to Mother.
    'Oh, how charming' said Mother, 'Thank you, dear husband.' She put her face close down to smell the fresh 'snowy' smell, and the thoughtful child couldn't help it – she put her arms round the Mother's neck.
The Thoughtful Child

THEY HAVE JUST TAKEN the new honey from the hives. I wish I could send you a jar. All the summer is shut up in a little pot. But summer is on the wane – the wane. Now Murry brings back autumn crocuses and his handkerchief is full of mushrooms. I love the satiny colour of mushrooms, & their *smell* & the soft stalk. The autumn crocuses push above short, mossy grass … And I feel as I always do that autumn is loveliest of all. There is such a sharpness with the sweetness – there is the sound of cold water running fast in the stream in the forest. Murry says the squirrels are tamer already. But Heavens Brett – Life is so marvellous, it is so rich – such a store of marvels that one can't say which one prefers.
Letter to Dorothy Brett, Chalet des Sapins, Montana-sur-Sierre, Switzerland, 29 August 1921

HORSE CHESTNUT *Aesculus hippocastanum*

THE TREES are budding almost before one's eyes in this warm weather – big white buds like birds in the chestnut trees, and round trees just sprinkled with green. The world is exceedingly lovely.
Notebook 18 (Notebooks, Volume One)

… I WENT to the Luxembourg gardens. About 3 of the biggest chestnut trees are really in leaf today – you never saw anything lovelier, with pigeons & babies adoring.
Letter to JMM, Paris, 21 March 1915

I cannot tell you how beautiful this place is by daylight. The trees on the island are in full leaf. I had quite forgotten the life that goes on *within* a tree – how it flutters and almost plumes itself and how the topmost branches tremble and the lowest branches of all swing lazy.
Letter to JMM, Paris, 6 May 1915

THIS EVENING I WENT walking in a park. Big drops splashed from the leaves and on the paths there lay a drift of pink and white chestnut flowers.
Letter to S S Koteliansky, Paris, 17 May 1915

… IN THE CAFÉS under the white & pink flowering chestnut trees there were more people & at the windows of the houses there were set pots of white narcissi and girls looked out … It was beyond words gay and delightful.
Letter to JMM, Clarens-Montreux, Switzerland, 15 May 1921

THE LITTLE TIGHT CHESTNUT buds that Jack stole from the Luxembourg Gardens have, in warm water and salt, swelled, abusted of themselves & turned into the most exquisite small dancing green stars. Too lovely for words.
Letter to Ida Baker, Paris, 8 April 1922

DAHLIA *Dahlia*

… THE SALLE À MANGER stretched before them. And the fifty little tables with the fifty pots of dahlias looked as if they might begin dancing …
Father and the Girls

THE FLOWERS are wonderful just now. Don't you love these real summer flowers? You should see the dahlias here, big spiky fellows, with buds like wax, and round white ones and real saffron yellow. The women are working in the vines. It's hot and fine with a light valley wind.
Letter to William Gerhardi, Sierre, Switzerland, 10 July 1922

SNAPDRAGON *Antirrhinum majus*

BY THE WAY this has been a marvellous year for dahlias. Do they grow well in Canada? We have saffron yellow, big spiked red ones, white ones and a little round bright orange kind – most lovely. As for the antirrhynms they are superb. I think I ought to have called them snap-dragons though. I'm sure that spelling is wrong. And do you grow zinnias? I wish I could see your garden. Dear little Jeanne seems to be a very fierce, successful gardener. We all as a family seem to inherit the tastes of our First Parents.
Letter to her sister Vera, Paris, 10 August 1922. The 'First Parents' were Adam and Eve in the Garden of Eden.

I had quite forgotten the life that goes on within a tree – how it flutters and almost plumes itself and how the topmost branches tremble and the lowest branches of all swing lazy

LESSER CELANDINE *Ficaria verna*

     … THERE'S A GOLD
Sheen on these flower petals as they fold
More truly mine, more like to my desire.

The flower petals fold. They are by the sun
Forgotten. In a shadowy wood they grow
Where the dark trees keep up a to-and-fro
Shadowy waving. Who will watch them shine
When I have dreamed my dream? Ah, darling mine!
Find them, gather them for me one by one.
Secret Flowers

AND THEN Arthur [Richard Murry] comes up from the field with a big bright celandine in his buttonhole. And you say as we go down, 'My God, there's a terrific lot to be done today'– but not as if you minded.
Letter to JMM, Bandol, France, 11 March 1918

PINK *Dianthus caryophyllus*

A STRANGE PINK like the eyes of white rabbits …
There is No Answer, Notebook 38

JAPONICA *Chaenomeles japonica*

WENT FOR A LITTLE WALK in the garden & saw all the pale violets. The beauty of palm trees. To fall in love with a tree … Japonica is a lovely flower, but people never grow enough of it.
Notebook 22 (Notebooks, Volume Two), 3 February 1920

THE PARIS GARDENS are simply a glorious sight with flowers – masses of beloved Japonica – enough Japonica at last.
Letter to JMM, Paris, 13 October 1922

Chalet des Sapins in Switzerland (*sapins*: firs).

EUROPEAN SILVER FIR *Abies alba*

WE ARE SO HIGH UP (5000 feet above the sea) that a cool breeze filters through from Heaven, and the forests are always airy … I can't imagine anything lovelier than this end of Switzerland. … Sierre, a little warm, sunripe town in the valley was so perfect that I felt I would like to live there. It has all the flowers of the South and it's gay and 'queynt' and full of nightingales. But since we have come up the mountains it seems lovelier still. We have taken a small not very small chalet here for two years. It is quite remote – in a forest clearing. The windows look over treetops across a valley to snowy peaks the other side. The air feels wonderful but smells more wonderful still. I have never lived *in* a forest before. One steps out of the house & in a moment one is hidden among the trees. And there are little glades and groves full of flowers, with small ice-cold streams twinkling through. It is my joy to sit there on a tree trunk …

    M. [Murry] and I live like two small timetables. We work all the morning & from tea to supper. After supper we read aloud and smoke; in the afternoon he goes walking & I crawling.
Letter to Ottoline Morrell, Chalet des Sapins, Montana-sur-Sierre, Switzerland, 24 July 1921

MONTANA is a small village (one street of new & ugly shops) on a plateau surrounded by mountains. It's 5000 feet high. Except for that street it's all fir and pine forests, little lawny pastures, ice-cold streams and air like old wine.
Letter to Sylvia Lynd, Chalet des Sapins, Montana-sur-Sierre, Switzerland, 24 September 1921

LITTLE ROUND BIRDS in the fir tree at the side window, scouring the tree for food. I crumbled a piece of bread but though the crumbs fell in the branches only two found them. There was a strange remoteness in the air, the scene, the winter cheeping … There was a great deal more snow this morning; it was very soft, 'like wool'. The coconut was bought and sawn in half and hung from J's balcony … Jack & I put out food for the birds. When I went to the window all the food was gone, but there was the tiny print of their feet on the sill. J. brought up the ½ coconut, and sprinkled crumbs as well. Very soon, terrified, however one came, then another, then a third balanced on the coconut. They are precious little atoms. It still snows.
Notebook 20 (Notebooks, Volume Two)

ZINNIA *Zinnia*

DID I TELL YOU I HAVE A LITTLE BOOKCASE made by a carpenter … His wife sent with it a bouquet of zinnias, the like of which I've never seen.
Letter to JMM, Isola Bella, Menton, 21 October 1920

I WANT SO MUCH to give you a little present before I leave here … And I have been casting about and I've nothing except this brand new little jacquette which is the colour of zinnias and reminds me of them. Would you like it?
Letter to 'Elizabeth' (Countess Russell), Sierre, 10 August 1922

V

Wild and windy Wellington

1906–1908

Back in Wellington in December 1906, after three stimulating years in the heart of London, KM found the contrast intolerable. Uprooted at eighteen, she hated her parents' stifling, conventional attitudes. 'Damn my family … What bores they are!' she wrote. She knew she *must* return to the more cultivated, intellectual and literary world of London.

Wellington's wind (and the battered chrysanthemums, roaring pine trees and 'savage' gorse-covered hills) matched KM's angry moods. Remembering her family's holiday cottage at Days Bay, she wrote in her draft story *Rewa*:

> At her touch the door burst open. With great difficulty she closed it again. And then the wind seemed to her like a giant child, waiting, watching for a moment's peephole to rush in – to invade the cottage, to blow it off the very face of the globe. There were no flowers left in the garden, and storm-beaten, her carnations and marigolds sprawled across the path. She … held to the fence …

But KM's mutinous months in Wellington were not idle. She took typing and book-keeping courses, practised her cello, and borrowed books by serious modern authors from the Parliamentary Library.

She was determined to be a writer. A few of her early efforts, such as *In the Botanical Gardens*, were published in the *Native Companion*, an Australian magazine. When she wrote to her editor she said she 'had a rapacious appetite for everything and principles as light as my purse'.

I woke and heard the wind moan and the roar
Of the dark water tumbling on the shore.

CHRYSANTHEMUM *Chrysanthemum x morifolium*

'OH, HEAVENS – this wind!' … Marie Swainson runs into the garden next door to pick the 'chrysanths' before they are ruined. Her skirt flies up above her waist; she tries to beat it down, to tuck it between her legs while she stoops, but it is no use – up it flies. All the trees and bushes beat about her. She picks as quickly as she can, but she is quite distracted. She doesn't mind what she does – she pulls the plants up by the roots and bends and twists them, stamping her foot and swearing.
The Wind Blows

THE VOICE of the chrysanthemum is heard in the land. Two blossoms – so full of colour that I feel they are lighting the dead summer on her journey – greet you from my table. Flowers like Tom's music seem to create in me a divine unrest – They revive strangely – dream memories – I know not what – They show me strange mystic paths – where perhaps I shall one day walk – To lean over a flower – as to hear any of his music is to suddenly [have] every veil torn aside – to commune soul with soul …
Letter to Vera Beauchamp, Wellington, March 1908

THE GARDEN BEDS were smothered … burning with the dusky fires of chrysanthemum blossoms.
Youth and Age

AND WE GREW so festive and gay that the rain outside
Sounded like dance music; the wild wind
Swept round the house like a friendly watch-dog …
To the child the chrysanthemum flower
Gave a little of her most delicious perfume.
The Earth Child, xxviii

CABBAGE TREE (TI KOUKA) *Cordyline australis*

OLD MR NEAVE stopped dead under a group of ancient cabbage palms outside the Government buildings! Enjoying himself! The wind of evening shook the dark leaves to a thin airy cackle.
An Ideal Family

THERE WAS A GREAT cabbage tree growing in the front garden and the shadow it cast on the door looked like a many-armed monster waving her away – the action was fantastic & real.
Notebook 29 (Notebooks, Volume One), April 1907

– TWO CABBAGE TREES stretched out phantom fingers –
Urewera Notebook (Esk Valley)

ABOVE THE CARPET BEDDING, on one hand, there is a green hedge, and above the hedge a long row of cabbage trees. I stare up at them, and, suddenly the green hedge is a stave, and the cabbage trees, now high, now low, have become an arrangement of notes – a curious, pattering, native melody.
In the Botanical Gardens

> Ruth Mantz was Katherine Mansfield's first biographer. She interviewed Millie Parker, a musician, who recalled spending a day with her friend KM in Wellington's Botanic Garden:
>
>> … We came to a new fence, I remember – upright posts at even intervals apart, and 5 rails across. Just in front of it a bed of young cabbage trees reared their round heads at varying heights. In a flash she saw it as a line of music, the fence the stave, the heads of the cabbage trees the notes, on the line and in the spaces. There being no clef mark, we hummed the melody through first as treble, then as bass, but found no tune either way, so it was put down as 'a strange native pattering melody.'
>
> *The Life of Katherine Mansfield,* by Ruth Elvish Mantz & J Middleton Murry

Wellington's Botanic Garden, main entrance. *Pinus radiata, Pinus sylvestris* and other conifers were grown there to assess their commercial potential.
FT series postcard

PINE *Pinus*

HE WAS A TALL, stately pine-tree. So tall, so very tall, that when you stood underneath and looked right up through the branches you could not see the top. How very fond you were of that pine-tree. We used to go and see it every day. He sang the most beautiful songs and told the most lovely stories; but he always seemed a little sad, somehow. You could not understand why for days and days, until one morning I discovered quite by accident – poor dear old pine-tree. No little bird had ever built a nest in his branches.
The Pine-Tree, The Sparrows, and You and I (Queen's College Magazine, 1903)

ON SUNDAY MORNINGS Pat, in the full glory of a clean blue shirt and corduroy trousers, took us for a walk in the great pine plantation … For years afterwards I believed that those trees just grew for the old witches of the woods, who used their needles in making the big, big umbrella over our heads, and all the dresses of the flowers, basting their nice, fine, blue sky calico with gum thoughtfully provided for them …
About Pat [Sheehan, the gardener] (Queen's College Magazine, 1905)

TRUTH TO TELL – I am just longing for the country – and especially for pine woods – they have a mystical fascination for me – but all trees have. Woods and the sea – both are perfect.
Letter to Sylvia Payne, London, 24 April 1906

THERE IS A LITTLE ASPHALT PATH like a mauve ribbon, and it is fringed with a vast procession of pine trees. In this dull light there seem to be hundreds of them. They are huddled together and muffled in their gloomy shadows.

On the earth a fragrant sweetness & pine needles, massed & heaped up, ruddy with perfume. And through the black lace-like tracery of trees a pale sky full of hurrying clouds. Far away in the distance a dreary waste of grey sea, a desert of heaving water.

Notebook 2 (Notebooks, Volume One), 1908

ON ONE SIDE of the hill grew a forest of pines from the road right down to the sea. On the other side short tufted grass and little bushes of white manuka flower. The pine-trees roared like waves in their topmost branches, their stems creaked like the timber of ships; in the windy air flew the white manuka flower. 'Ah-k!' shouted Ole Underwood, shaking his umbrella at the wind bearing down upon him, beating him, half strangling him with his black cape. 'Ah-k!' shouted the wind a hundred times as loud …

Ole Underwood

I WENT into Jinnie's garden & lay all the morning under the pine trees. To have all that overgrown half run wild garden has simply *intoxicated* me. I found it this morning. It was like a better Karori.

Letter to JMM, Isola Bella, Menton, 25 September 1920

PLAYTIME came and Isabel was surrounded … She held quite a court under the huge pine trees at the side of the playground …

… Even the dinner hour was given up to talking about it [the doll's house]. The little girls sat under the pines eating their thick mutton sandwiches and big slabs of johnny cake spread with butter.

The Doll's House

FLAX (HARAKEKE) *Phormium tenax*

WIND RAISES great pillars of sand up in the road, in the bush, the trees lashing together, and the long leaves of the flax bushes stream like ribbons of green & silver.

Rewa

MANUKA *Leptospermum scoparium*

IN A STEAMER CHAIR, under a manuka tree that grew in the middle of the front grass patch, Linda Burnell dreamed the morning away. She did nothing. She looked up at the dark, close, dry leaves of the manuka, at the chinks of blue between, and now and again a tiny yellowish flower dropped on her. Pretty – yes, if you held one of those flowers on the palm of your hand and looked at it closely, it was an exquisite small thing. Each pale yellow petal shone as if each was the careful work of a loving hand. The tiny tongue in the centre gave it the shape of a bell.
At the Bay (VI)

WE PASSED over oily thick green lake – round the sides the manuka clambered in fantastic blossoming – the air is heavy with sulphur …
Urewera Notebook (Waiotapu)

… & THERE, just on the bank the flowering manuka is a riot of white colour against the blue water – a lark sings – the water bubbles …
Urewera Notebook (Waikato River)

I STAND in the manuka scrub, the fairy blossom – Away ahead the pines – black, the soughing of the wind.
Urewera Notebook (Taupo)

FENNEL *Foeniculum vulgare*

THEY CANNOT WALK fast enough. Their heads bent, their legs just touching, they stride like one eager person through the town, down the asphalt zigzag where the fennel grows wild and on to the esplanade. It is dusky – just getting dusky. The wind is so strong that they have to fight their way through it, rocking like two old drunkards.
The Wind Blows

JERUSALEM CHERRY *Solanum pseudocapsicum*

TALL BUSHES overhung the stream with red leaves and dazzling yellow flowers and clusters of red and white berries, and a little further on there were cresses and a water plant with a flower like a yellow foxglove.
The Aloe. The water plant described was the yellow monkey flower.

LAST NIGHT for the first time since you were dead
I walked with you, my brother, in a dream.
We were at home again beside the stream
Fringed with tall berry bushes, white and red.
'Don't touch them: they are poisonous,' I said.
But your hand hovered, and I saw a beam
Of strange bright laughter flying round your head
And as you stooped I saw the berries gleam –
'Don't you remember? We called them Dead Man's Bread!'
I woke and heard the wind moan and the roar
Of the dark water tumbling on the shore.
Where – where is the path of my dream for my eager feet?
By the remembered stream my brother stands
Waiting for me with berries in his hands
'These are my body. Sister, take and eat.'
To L.H.B. (1894–1915)

GORSE *Ulex europaeus*

AGAINST THE PEARL SKY the great hills tower, gorse-covered, leonine, magnificently savage. The air is quiet with thin rain, yet, from the karaka tree comes a tremulous sound of bird song.
Unbound paper

WHEN SHE PULLED up the blind next morning the trees outside were being tossed to and fro, and the sea lashed into fury by a wild Southerly gale … in the afternoon [she] put on her reefer coat & tam-o'-shanter and went for a walk up the hills that spread like a great wall behind the little town. The wind blew fiercer than ever. She held on to bushes and strong tufts of grass, and climbed rapidly, rejoicing in the strength that it required. Down in the hollow where the gorse spread like a thick green mantle she paused to recover breath. The utter loneliness of it filled her with pleasure. She stood perfectly still, letting the wind blow cold & strong in her face and loosen her hair.
Juliet

THEN ALL IN A FEVER myself I rushed out of the stifling house – out of the city streets and on to the gorse golden hills. A white road ran round the hills – there I walked. And below me, like a beautiful Pre-Raphaelite picture, lay the sea and the violet mountains. The sky all a riot of rose and yellow, amethyst and purple.
Vignette: Through the Autumn Afternoon (Wellington)

A STRETCH of gorse clothing the hillside has caught fire.
    From my window I see the blue smoke spreading afar in twists and turns and curves of thin exquisite loveliness. I see, too, the fierce red glow of the flames. I watch their mad hungry progress. There is a steady, strong destructive sound. The flames rush forward, crying, 'See, see, can we *ever* be satisfied.'
L'Incendie, Unbound papers (Notebooks, Volume One), 21 January 1907

POHUTUKAWA *Metrosideros excelsa*

ALL THE POOR little pohutukawas on the esplanade are bent to the ground.
The Wind Blows

VI

Away to the bush gloried hills

November–December 1907

Most of Wellington's hills were bare of trees by the 1890s, when Katherine Mansfield was growing up. She did not mention ngaio, taupata or rangiora, small natives that were common in Wellington gardens and roadsides, and nor did she describe kowhai, even though a yellow kowhai flower was found pressed between the pages of one of her notebooks. However, she observed other free-standing native trees: karaka, pohutukawa, lacebark and cabbage trees. She loved manuka, and the clumps of graceful toetoe and flax which grew in open country. She sometimes climbed through the bush on the hills behind Eastbourne, but apart from bush lawyer, supplejack and bright red rata she knew very few names — for her bush was just bush.

In November 1907 KM joined a group in Napier and spent a month exploring parts of New Zealand, including some seldom visited. Horses pulled their covered wagons up the Napier–Taupo road to the volcanic plateau, and turned north at Rangitaiki to follow an indistinct track through golden tussock over the Kaingaroa Plains to remote Murupara. They slept in tents beside isolated Maori settlements, and drove through 'passionately secret' bush in the Urewera country where KM was awed by the 'gigantic and tragic' landscape.

The *Urewera Notebook* records her interest in colourful berries and flowers — konini, rata and mistletoe. In the 'bush gloried hills' she plucked sprays of white native clematis. She admired tree ferns such as ponga and mamaku, and the 'amazingly emerald' tutu, but did not identify any of the forest giants of the Urewera bush, not even prominent trees such as rimu or rewarewa.

After the Urewera expedition, the party turned west to visit the thermal wonders of Rotorua, and returned to Napier via Taupo.

The Woman at the Store was inspired by this extraordinary expedition. Six months later, at nineteen, KM left New Zealand for good.

TOETOE *Austroderia fulvida*

A HEAVY DEW had fallen. The grass was blue. Big drops hung on the bushes and just did not fall; the silvery, fluffy toi-toi was limp on its long stalks, and all the marigolds and the pinks in the bungalow gardens were bowed to the earth with wetness. Drenched were the cold fuchsias, round pearls of dew lay on the flat nasturtium leaves. It looked as though the sea had beaten up softly in the darkness, as though one immense wave had come rippling, rippling – how far?
At the Bay (1)

BELOW US … a clump of toi-toi waving in the wind – & looking for all the world – like a family of little girls drying their hair …
Urewera Notebook (Kaitoke)

MIST OVER the distant hills – the fascinating valleys of toi toi swayed by the wind. Silence again, and a wind full of the loneliness and the sweetness of the wild places …
Urewera Notebook (Rotorua)

THE RAIN had ceased … The sky was faintly mirrored in the yellow puddles. On both sides of the road the toi toi branches bent in the wind to shake out their fluffy golden hair. She had never seen the bush more exquisite.
Rewa

SUN ORCHID (MAIKAIKA) *Thelymitra*

ALL THAT DAY the heat was terrible. The wind blew close to the ground – it rooted among the tussock grass – slithered along the road, so that the white pumice dust swirled in our faces – settled and sifted over us and was like a dry-skin itching for growth on our bodies … There was nothing to be seen but wave after wave of tussock grass – patched with purple orchids and manuka bushes covered with thick spider webs.
The Woman at the Store

TUSSOCK (WI) *Chionochloa rubra*

KATHIE IN THE MORNING in the manuka paddock saw the dew hanging from the blossoms – & leaves – put it to her lips – & it seemed to poison her with the longing for the sweet wildness of the plains – for the silent speech of the Silent Places – the golden sea of tussock.
Urewera Notebook

BUSH — TE WAO NUI A TANE

AND, SUDDENLY, it disappears – all the pretty, carefully-tended surface of gravel and sward and blossom, and there is bush, silent and splendid. On the green moss, on the brown earth, a wide splashing of yellow sunlight. And, everywhere that strange, indefinable scent. As I breathe it, it seems to absorb, to become part of me – and I am old with the age of centuries, strong with the strength of savagery.
In the Botanical Gardens

KM's group on the road between Te Whaiti and Ruatahuna in the Urewera, 1907. George Ebbett is driving the covered wagon in front, with HJ and Elsie Webber in the luggage wagon behind.
Alexander Turnbull Library F2588 1/2

A typical New Zealand bush scene.
Garth Baker

ALL THE WHARES look out upon the river and the valley and the bush gloried hills. These trees smothered in cream blossom.
Urewera Notebook

FROM THIS SADDLE we look across mile upon mile of green bush then brown bush russet colour – blue distance – and a wide cloud flecked sky … Once at the head of a great valley – the blazing sun uplifts itself like a gigantic torch to light the bush – it is all so gigantic – and tragic – even in the bright sunlight it is so passionately secret … A green-red & brown butterfly, the green hill in vivid sunlight & then a vault of green bush the sunlight slanting in to the trees – an island in the river decked with tree fern – And always through the bush – this hushed sound of water running – on brown pebbles – it seems to breathe the full deep – bygone essence of it all …
Urewera Notebook (near Te Whaiti)

On the edge of the Urewera, near Lake Waikaremoana, 2016.
Harald Selke

EVERYWHERE ON THE HILLS – great masses of charred logs – looking for
all the world like strange fantastic beasts – a yawning crocodile, a headless
horse – a gigantic gosling – a watchdog – to be smiled at and scorned in the
daylight – but a veritable nightmare in the darkness – and now & again the
silver tree trunks – like a skeleton army, invade the hills …
Urewera Notebook

In the savage heart of the bush
The tui lifts her white throat
Three bell-like notes – then the answer she knows so well
And sings for herself – the love answer of laughter.
The Earth Child, xxvii

BUSH LAWYER (TATARAMOA) *Rubus cissoides*
SUPPLEJACK (KAREAO) *Ripogonum scandens*

ONCE IN THE BUSH it was easier – she was more sheltered, though the sound
was more violent. It seemed that every tree had found voice … She climbed
quickly, catching at trees & branches, wrenching her hand. A long arm
of lawyer pulled her skirt – the leaves brilliantly scarlet, the plant looked

as though it had fed on blood. Sticking to the supplejacks, almost swinging herself upwards. And at last the top was reached & the bush behind. She slipped onto the grass plateau, the great ledge overhanging the sea – here, unprotected, the wind spent its fury …
Rewa

… A WEIRD PASSIONATE abandon of birds – the bush birds' cries – the fanciful shapes of the supplejacks …
Urewera Notebook

SILVER FERN (PONGA)
Cyathea dealbata

THE FERN TREES built in the blue air
Their canopy of silver and green.
The Earth Child, viii

NOW THEY COULD SEE, quite plainly, dark bush. Even the shapes of the umbrella ferns showed, and those strange silvery withered trees that are like skeletons …
The Voyage

THEN THROUGH MORE BUSH – the ferns are almost too exquisite – gloomy shades – sequestered deeps – & out again …
Urewera Notebook

'SEE THE HANGING beautiful arms of the fern trees,' laughed Hinemoa.
　'Not arms, not arms [said Marina]. All the other trees have arms – saving the rata with its tongues of flame – but the fern trees have beautiful green hair …'
Summer Idyll

CLEMATIS (PUAWANANGA) *Clematis paniculata*
CLIMBING RATA *Metrosideros fulgens*
NEW ZEALAND MISTLETOE (PIRITA) *Peraxilla colensoi*

… [WE] DIVED down a bridle track – and followed the bush – The tuis really sounded like rivers running – everywhere the trees hung wreathed with clematis – and rata and mistletoe – It was very cool & we washed in a creek – the sides all smothered in daisies – the ferns everywhere …

We got great sprays of clematis – and Konini, and drove first through a bush path – But the greatest sight I have seen was the view from the top of Taranga-Kuma – You draw rein at the top of the mountains & round you everywhere are other mountains – bush covered – & far below in the valley little Tarawera & a silver ribbon of river –

Urewera Notebook (unsent letter to Annie Beauchamp, describing the bush near Te Pohue and beside the Napier–Taupo road, 26 November 1907)

RATA *Metrosideros robusta*

THEY REACHED THE ISLAND & lay on a long smooth ledge of brown rock & rested. Above them the fern trees rose, & among the fern trees a rata rose like a pillar of flame.

Summer Idyll

HONEYSUCKLE *Lonicera japonica*

WE WAKE EARLY – and wash and dress – & go down to bath again – Honeysuckle – roses pink & white – periwinkles syringas – red hot pokers – those *yellow flowers* – the ground is smothered – Fruit trees with promise of harvest … I feel I cannot leave but pluck the honeysuckle…
Urewera Notebook (Terraces Hotel, Taupo)

BRIAR ROSE *Rosa rubiginosa*
WILLOW *Salix*

… THE BIRDS – the wonderful green flax swamp, and always these briars … The Hamurana Spring the still rain – the colour – the tangle of willow & rose & thorn – like Millais' Ophelia the undergrowth – & then the spring …
Urewera Notebook (Rotorua)

BEFORE THEM a wide sheet of swift smooth water … the willow tree – shaggy and laden dips lazily luxuriously in the water …
Urewera Notebook (Waikato River)

TODAY WAS PERFECT perfect – I leaned out of the window after you had gone and watched the willows flying in the sun.
Letter to Ottoline Morrell, Hampstead, 7 June 1919

HOW BEAUTIFUL willows are – how beautiful – how the sun rains down upon them – the tiny leaves move like fishes.
Letter to Dorothy Brett, Hampstead, 18 July 1919

BROOM *Cytisus scoparius*

THEN WE ARE IN A VALLEY of broom – such colour – it is strewn everywhere – I have never dreamed of such vivid blossom –
Urewera Notebook (near Rangitaiki)

O VALLEY of waving broom,
O lovely, lovely light,
O heart of the world, red-gold!
Breast high in the blossom I stand;
It beats about me like waves
Of a magical, golden sea.

The barren heart of the world
Alive at the kiss of the sun,
The yellow mantle of Summer
Flung over a laughing land,
Warm with the warmth of her body,
Sweet with the kiss of her breath.

O valley of waving broom,
O lovely, lovely light,
O mystical marriage of Earth
With the passionate Summer sun!
To her lover she holds a cup
And the yellow wine o'erflows.
He has lighted a little torch
And the whole of the world is ablaze.
Prodigal wealth of love!
Breast high in the blossom I stand.
In the Rangitaiki Valley

THE TASSELS of the broom swept the long hillside …
The Earth Child, viii

AWAY AHEAD – in the silver sea lies the island – Then the wild sky – everywhere the golden broom tossed its golden fragrant plumes into the evening air.
Urewera Notebook (near Taupo)

VII

England through the seasons

1908–1922

When KM was nineteen her father Harold paid for her one-way passage to London, and provided a regular allowance. Very soon her 'rapacious appetite' for experience resulted in several unwise relationships, an unconsummated marriage, a miscarriage and venereal disease, which led to crippling attacks of rheumatism. In 1909 Annie Beauchamp cut her out of her will, although the allowance from Harold continued. A hint of her mother's harshness appears in *Prelude*: Linda 'particularly liked the long sharp thorns that edged the aloe.'

The worst blow fell in 1917, when KM learned she had tuberculosis. But through all these painful, turbulent years she worked at her writing. She found English publishers: *In a German Pension* came out in 1911, *Prelude* in 1918, *Bliss* in 1921, *The Garden Party* in 1922.

In England, in spite of her failing health, KM achieved the intellectual life she needed. She mixed with editors, critics and writers, among them John Middleton Murry, D H Lawrence, Virginia Woolf, Bertrand Russell, Aldous Huxley, Walter de la Mare, James Joyce and T S Eliot. She made friends with the artists Anne Estelle Rice (later Drey) and Dorothy Brett. Many of these people belonged to the Bloomsbury set, who often spent weekends at Garsington, the country home of Lady Ottoline Morrell.

The portrait by Anne Rice (1918) reflects KM's enduring passion for flowers — together they admired a beautiful poppy with a 'marvellous black sheen at the base of the petal and the big purplish centre'. When she saw hawthorn in bloom she wrote that the countryside was 'simply bowed down with beauty … the wild flowers are in such profusion that it's almost agony to see them.' However, in May 1919, a year after her marriage to Murry, and feeling ill, quarrelsome and rejected, she wrote, 'I would not care if I never saw the English country again. Even in its flowering I feel deeply antagonistic to it

& I will never change. [Murry is] of one nation, I of another …' This mood did lift — KM and Murry were soon planning to buy a country cottage, pre-naming it The Heron, after her dead brother Leslie Heron Beauchamp. She wanted to write more about their shared New Zealand childhood, keeping precious memories in print and alive: 'I hear his voice in trees and flowers, in scents and light and shadow' (late 1915, *Notebooks, Volume Two*).

Although Murry bought a cottage in a Sussex village near Lewes, she was never well enough to live there.

ABOVE KM's brother Leslie Beauchamp, shortly before he died in Belgium in 1915.

RIGHT KM with Leslie and her sister Jeanne in Wellington, 1907.
Alexander Turnbull Library, F112213 1/2; 1/2-011986-F

I hear his voice in trees and flowers, in scents and light and shadow

SPRING

HAWTHORN (MAY) *Crataegus monogyna*

I HAD A VERY COMFORTABLE JOURNEY – The country, in the bright swooning light was simply bowed down with beauty, heavy, weighed down with treasure – Shelley's moonlight may glittered everywhere, the wild flowers are in such a profusion that it's almost an agony to see them and know that they are there – I have never seen anything more solemn and splendid than England in May […]– why is our youth passing while the world renews itself in its glory!
Letter to JMM, Cornwall, 17 May 1918 – in a letter on 18 February 1918 she had written 'Isn't that lovely where Shelley speaks of the 'moonlight-coloured may'?'

… ALL EARLY SPRING plants and so on are extremely hardy. It is not they who come to harm. Bitterest cold, east wind, and storm won't hurt violets or hawthorn buds or daffodils or primroses. They seem to have some special resisting power in these months. Even half open leaves can stand snow.
Letter to Ida Baker, Paris, 2 April 1922

GILLYFLOWER *Dianthus caryophyllus*

ANNE & I have been sitting outside – she talking about the spring – She can't mention the flowers without her eyes just *cry over* as she says – She brought me masses of pink lupins – terrifying flowers – but beautiful. The garden is so gay with real purple columbines and gillyflowers and marigolds – and early roses …
Letter to JMM, Cornwall, 22 May 1918

PRIMROSE *Primula vulgaris*

A GIRL PASSED under my window this morning selling primroses. I bought great bunches of them, and untied their tight chains, and let them stretch their poor little tired cramped selves in a sky-blue dish that had been filled with primroses every year. But they were not like country primroses.
My Potplants

HENRY LAY on his back in the little wood. When he moved the dead leaves rustled beneath him, and above his head the new leaves quivered like fountains of green water steeped in sunlight. Somewhere out of sight Edna was gathering primroses. He had been so full of dreams that morning that he could not keep pace with her delight in the flowers.

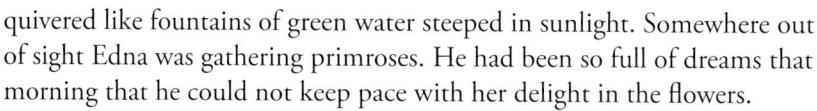

… 'Oh, Henry – such beauties! I've never seen such beauties. Come and look.' … Henry knelt down by her and took some primroses out of her basket and made a long chain to go round her throat.
Something Childish But Very Natural, VI

THERE IS A CREEK close by our house that rushes down a narrow valley and then falls down a steep cliff into the sea – The banks are covered with primroses & violets and bluebells.
Letter to Beatrice Campbell, Cornwall, 4 May 1916

NOW I HAVE ARRIVED at the word 'Primroses' & I see them. Delicate pinkish stems, and the earthy feeling as one picks them so close to the damp soil. I love their leaves too, and I like to kiss buds of primroses. One could kiss them away. They feel so marvellous.
Letter to Dorothy Brett, Paris, 26 February 1922

the shadows raced over the silky grass
& the cuckoos sang

BLUEBELL *Hyacinthoides non-scripta*

BUT WHAT ABOUT BLUEBELLS. Oh dear! Bluebells are just as good [as primroses]. White ones, faint blue ones that grow in shady hollows, very dark blue ones, pale ones. I had one whole spring full of bluebells one year with [D H] Lawrence. I shall never forget it. And it was warm, not very sunny, the shadows raced over the silky grass & the cuckoos sang.
Letter to Dorothy Brett, Paris, 26 February 1922

IT WAS VERY HOT – all glowing & quiet with loud birds singing & the bluebells smelled like honey … We drove through lanes like great flowery loops with the sea below and huge gulls sailing over … until we came to this hotel which stands in its garden facing the open sea.
Letter to JMM, Cornwall, 17 May 1918

IT IS A PALE English day – more silver than white. The cook has brought me in a bunch of bluebells. How lovely they are, these flowers of the wood. They have a sweet smell, and like all these early spring flowers as one touches them one thinks of water.
Letter to Sydney & Violet Schiff, Hampstead, London, 10 May 1920

IRIS *Iris pseudacorus*

ANNE & DREY [Anne Rice and her husband] came in last evening with an armful of those yellow irises that grew in the Marsh near Hockings Farm. They had been picnicking in the woods all day among the bluebells & were very burnt and happy.
Letter to JMM, Cornwall, 19 May 1918

EVERY BLADE – every twig has come into flower – Right down by the sea there are the foxgloves, sea pinks, dog daisies – I even found violets – and yellow irises everywhere …
Letter to JMM, Cornwall, 1 June 1918

SUMMER

CAMPION *Silene dioica*

WHAT A DAY to be born!
And what a place!
Cried the flowers …
The campions, the bluebells
The daisies and buttercups
The bright little eyebright and the white nettle flower
And a thousand others,
All were there to greet her –
And growing so high – so high
(Right up to the sky, thought the butterfly)
On either side of a little lane.
The Butterfly

EYEBRIGHT
Euphrasia officinalis

NETTLE *Urtica dioica*

BUT I TELL YOU, MY LORD FOOL,
OUT OF THIS NETTLE, DANGER,
WE PLUCK THIS FLOWER, SAFETY.

This Shakespearean quotation was much loved by Katherine Mansfield and is inscribed on her grave at Fontainebleau:
Henry IV Part 1, Act 2, Scene 3

FOXGLOVE *Digitalis purpurea*

ALWAYS, when I see foxgloves, I think of the Lawrences. Again I pass in front of their cottage and in the window, between the daffodil curtains with the green spots – there are the great, sumptuous blooms.

'And how beautiful they are against whitewash' cry the Lawrences. As is their custom, when they love anything, they make a sort of Festa. With foxgloves everywhere. And then they sit in the middle of them, like blissful prisoners, dining in an encampment of Indian Braves.
Remembrance. Festa means festival.

BUT WAIT until you see [in Cornwall] the yellow irises & the foxgloves over 6 foot high – red indian encampments of foxgloves burning with passion & pride in the field next to yours.
Letter to Virginia Woolf, Hampstead, London, 5 May 1919

HEATHER *Calluna vulgaris*

IN THE PURPLE HEATHER
We lay like two gods on sun-flushed cloud pillows.
We could not see each other – so deep and thick our beds,
And therefore we talked heart-to-heart, like lovers on a night journey.
The Earth Child, xxv

AUTUMN

OH EARTH! Lovely, unforgettable Earth! Yesterday I saw the leaves falling, so gently, so softly, raining down from little slender trees golden against the blue. Perhaps Autumn is loveliest. Lo! it is Autumn. What is the magic of that? It is magic to me.
Letter to JMM, Paris, 13 October 1922

IN THE AUTUMN garden leaves falling. Like footfalls, like gentle whispering. They fly, spin, twirl, shake.
Journal, 18 October 1922

THE LEAVES are falling on Hampstead Heath, lifting, spinning, flying, tossing, dancing, chasing, but falling falling. It is very cold …

A soldier & a girl come walking … There is a loud roaring in the trees, & away the leaves fly. She catches one & shuts it up in her fist & he opens the little hand finger by finger & there is the leaf inside. At the sight of the little hand outspread with the leaf on it his heart grows big.
Love in autumn, Unbound Papers, 1918

LONDON PLANE *Platanus x acerifolia*

A SUDDEN BREEZE in the Square caught the leaves of the plane trees, burnt a bright golden and a dull brown, and whirled them into the air like a flock of magic birds.
The Education of Audrey

VIRGINIA CREEPER
Parthenocissus tricuspidata

OVER THE WHITE HOUSE a Virginia creeper has run like a thin sheet of flame, and when she saw the sumac tree in the avenue – 'I would like to warm my hands there, Father, it would nearly make toast.'
The Thoughtful Child: In Autumn

THE VIRGINIA CREEPER, like blood, streams down the face of the houses.
October (to V.M.B.)

MICHAELMAS DAISY
Aster amellus

YOUTH AND AGE walked hand in hand beneath the trees. A strange, half-frozen day, yet the air was drenched with thin sunshine, and the blue sky full of white winged clouds … The garden beds were smothered under a mauve mist of Michaelmas daisies, burning with the dusky fires of chrysanthemum blossoms.
Youth and Age

THEY ARE WALKING up and down the garden in Acacia Road. It is dusky; the Michaelmas daisies are as bright as feathers.
Unbound papers (Notebooks, Volume Two), October 1915

MICHAELMAS DAISIES remind me of a solitary bush in Acacia Road. Do you remember? I like them. They have such very delicate arrowy petals.
Letter to JMM, Paris, 14 October 1922

WINTER

HAWTHORN BERRY *Crataegus monogyna*

MY BIRD, my darling,
Calling through the cold of afternoon –
Those round, bright notes,
Each one so perfect
Shaken from the other and yet
Hanging together in flashing clusters!
The small soft flowers and the ripe fruit
All are gathered.
It is the season now of nuts and berries
And round bright flashing drops
On the frozen grass.
Winter Bird

HAZEL NUT *Corylus avellana*

HOLLY *Ilex aquifolium*

SHALL WE NEXT YEAR really keep Christmas? *Shall* we have a tree & put it in a room with the door locked – only you and I allowed to go in & decorate it – & then have a small party on Christmas Eve?? We shall go out all wrapped up to the noses, with a pruning hook to cut holly & we'll burn a Christmas log.
*Letter to JMM, Ospedaletti, Italy,
30 November 1919*

IVY *Hedera helix*

SNOW – heavy snow over everything. The lawn is covered with a wavy pattern of cat's paws; there is a thick, thick icing on the garden table; the withered pods of the laburnum tree are white tassels; only here and there in the ivy is a dark leaf showing.
The Man without a Temperament

HE PUTS HIS ARM round her. They pace up and down. A thin round moon shines over the pear tree & the ivy walls of the garden glitter like metal. The air smells chill, heavy, very cold …

   Their shadows on the grass are long & strange. A puff of strange wind whispers in the ivy and the old moon touches them with silver. She shivers.
Unbound papers; Notebooks, Volume Two, October 1915

SNOWDROP *Galanthus nivalis*

IT'S JUST TWO MONTHS to Christmas, after that the New Year, & in February snowdrops – and they are the flowers of *our* spring.
Letter to JMM, Ospedaletti, Italy, 23 October 1919

DURING MY CHILDHOOD I lived surrounded by a luxurious quantity of flowers, and they were my only companions. My Mother died when I was very young and I had no brothers or sisters. How I loved my life. My greatest delight then was to find fresh flowers to love, and my greatest sorrow if they should die. I remember the year when Spring was very late in coming. I had stolen out in the garden in the dead of night to cover with a blanket the little snowdrop I had found the day before.
My Potplants

VIII

The warm, fragrant Mediterranean

1915–1921

Early in 1915 when Leslie Beauchamp arrived in England to take an officer's training course, KM began to write *The Aloe*, the first version of *Prelude*, about her Karori childhood. After Leslie was killed in October, KM retreated in grief to Bandol in the south of France, accompanied for a while by Murry, and worked on the story. She relished the special fragrances of the Mediterranean: her *Notebooks* mention 'the wild spicy scent of the rosemary', 'the white waxy scent that lay upon the jonquil fields' and 'the smell of the full summer sea and the bay tree in the garden and the smell of lemons'.

Menton, on the Mediterranean in France. The Villa Isola Bella is at the front right.
Stuart Hoar

Katherine Mansfield at the Villa Isola Bella.
Ida Baker photo, Alexander Turnbull Library 1/2-011912-F

When tuberculosis was diagnosed in late 1917, KM again journeyed south to Bandol to escape the English winter. Ida Baker decided that her friend was too ill to manage alone and followed her. In March 1918 they struggled back to London together, becoming trapped in Paris for three weeks by a major German bombardment. In the autumn of 1919 KM stayed on the Italian Riviera with the faithful Ida, who at times enraged her, but on whose practical help she depended. Although she was so ill, nature still delighted her: 'The sea dances, the olives dance with tiny flickering leaves.'

In January 1920 she was cared for by a cousin in Menton in France. The next winter KM returned with Ida to Menton, where she was charmed by the Villa Isola Bella. She loved its feathery date palms and scented orange blossom. She told Murry, 'I could weep for joy', and he joined her there.

By June 1921 all three had moved to Switzerland, hoping KM's health would improve in the clean mountain air. She appreciated the geraniums in her chalet window — 'their rosy masses of flowers against the blue space are wonderful.' In spite of her advanced tuberculosis she managed to finish some of her finest stories, among them *The Garden Party*, *At the Bay*, *The Voyage*, *The Doll's House* and *The Fly*.

An attempt to find a cure in France proved futile, and Mansfield died at Fontainebleau, near Paris, on 9 January 1923, aged 34.

CANARY DATE PALM *Phoenix canariensis*

THIS LITTLE PLACE is and always will be for me the one and only place, I feel. My heart beats for it like it beats for Karori […] Walking on the terrace by starlight looking up through my vieux palmier [old palm tree] I could weep for joy. Running into the garden to see how many more buds are out in the morning is to run straight at – into – a blessing.

… You will find ISOLA BELLA in poker work on my heart. …
Letters to JMM, Isola Bella, Menton, 10 and 12 November 1920

HER LITTLE HOT ROOM looked over the bay
Through a stiff palisade of glinting palms,
And there she would lie in the heat of the day,
Her dark head resting upon her arms,
So quiet, so still, she did not seem
To think, to feel, or even to dream.
Sanary

– LOOKED UP and saw an old female leaning on a broom watching me & smiling very broadly … Her broom by the way, was made of those great reddish stems that grow in the centre of palms with tiny dates on them – a very nice broom indeed.
Letter to JMM, Ospedaletti, Italy, 24 November 1919

I WENT OUT into the garden just now. It is starry and mild. The leaves of the palm are like down-drooping feathers; the grass looks soft, unreal, like moss.
Notebook 35 (Notebooks, Volume Two), 27 December 1920

THE WIND still blows a hurricane here … If a window is opened the seas of the air rush in & fill it. Two great palm trees have snapped like corks & many a glittering plume trails in the dust.
Letter to JMM, Bandol, France, 22 January 1918

'HERE' IS A ROOM with the window opening on to a balcony & below the balcony there is a small tree full of tangerines and beyond the tree a palm and beyond the palm a long garden with a great tangled – it looks like – a wood at the bottom of it. *Palms* … are superb things. Their colour is amazing. Sometimes they are bronze – sometimes gold and green – warm deep tiger-gold – & last night, under the moon in a little window they were bright silver. And plus that the creatures are full of drawing. How marvellous life is – if only one gives oneself up to it! It seems to me that the *secret* of life is to *accept* life … It's only by risking losing yourself – giving yourself up to Life – that you can ever find out the answer.
Letter to Richard Murry, L'Hermitage, Menton, 25 January 1920

BLUE GUM *Eucalyptus globulus*

IT WAS BRIGHT with sun. The palm-trees stood up into the air, crisp and shining; the blue gums hung heavy with sun as is their wont.
Unbound papers (Notebooks, Volume Two), late 1915

VERY STUBBORN and solid are the trunks of the palm trees. Springing from their tops the stiff green bouquets seem to cut into the evening air and, among them, the blue gum trees, tall and slender with sickle-shaped leaves and drooping branches half blue, half violet.
Et in Arcadia Ego

… AND THE GUM-leaves, like tufts of cock's feathers ruffled in the faint breeze.
Notebook 36 (Notebooks, Volume Two)

THEN SOMETHING IMMENSE came into view; an enormous shock-haired giant with his arms stretched out. It was the big gum-tree outside Mrs Stubbs's shop, and as they passed by there was a strong whiff of eucalyptus.
At the Bay (1)

The blue gum trees … with sickle-shaped leaves and drooping branches …

JONQUIL *Narcissus*

YESTERDAY AFTERNOON I walked to Sanary … There is a long beach there too and on the other side of the road fields of jonquils in flower. Two women … with black straw hats were picking them. As I passed they stood up & held the big nodding bunches before their eyes to see who was passing. There is a tiny villa there, too … Behind it rears up an old rock covered with that pink heath & rosemary.
Letter to JMM, Bandol, France, 9 December 1915

YESTERDAY I WENT for a long walk round by the sea … & then I struck inland & came home by little lanes & crooked ways bordered with olive trees – past the flower farms … I got quite lost … when I peered through the gates there was never a soul to be seen except jonquils & daffodils & big blue violets & white roses.
Letter to JMM, Bandol, France, 10 December 1915

… STILL TO SMELL the white waxy scent that lay upon the jonquil fields …
Et in Arcadia Ego

THE WHITE, white fields of Jonquil flowers
Danced up as high as her knee
And flashed and sparkled before her eyes
Until she could hardly see.
So to the woods went she.
The Town between the Hills

GOOD MORNING, my darling. There's a debonaire wind blowing today and a very pale, faint jonquil sun.
Letter to JMM, Isola Bella, Menton, 4 November 1920

THERE IS A NEW SORT of jonquil here that I must find out the name of. We must grow it. It's so lovely – and the green is very deep, the flower very starry. You see our future is so miraculous – so delicate – so heavenly – that how can one help trembling – & feeling terrified when this great blast roars between us and it.
Letter to JMM, Bandol, France, 12-13 February 1918

OLIVE *Olea europaea*

THE SEA DANCES, the olives dance with tiny flickering leaves … The olives are ripe and beginning to fall.
Letter to JMM, Ospedaletti, Italy, 6-7 October 1919

YESTERDAY I WENT for a long scrambling walk in the woods – on the other side of the railway. There are no roads there – just little tracks & old mule paths. Parts are quite wild and overgrown, then in all sorts of unexpected faery places you find a little clearing – the ground cultivated in tiny red terraces & sheltered by olive trees (full of tiny black fruit). There grow the jonquils, daffodils, new green peas and big abundant rose bushes … Once I found myself right at the very top of a hill and below there lay an immense valley – surrounded by mountains – very high ones & it was so clear you could see every pointed pine, every little zig-zag track – the black stems of the olives showing sooty and soft among the silvery green – One could see for miles and miles … Oh, Bogey, how I longed for my playfellow.
Letter to JMM, Bandol, France, 22 December 1915

REALLY WHEN YOU COME in May … [we will] see this little house as I did perched on the hill half in sun half swept by the dancing shadow of the olive trees – And there will be flowers everywhere –
Letter to JMM, Ospedaletti, Italy, 11 October 1919

BUT BOGEY I do so long for you to know this country in the spring. It's like the Middle Ages, somehow … driving up those valleys & seeing the great shower of flowers & seeing the dark silver olives & the people working in the bean fields – one feels as though one were part of the *tradition* of spring –
Letter to JMM, Villa Flora, Menton, 12 April 1920

ORANGE *Citrus sinensis*

… MAY HAS BROUGHT me a big branch of orange blossom all wet with rain …

There is a piece of orange blossom for you [sketch] buds & leaves – but oh! I can't draw the scent.
Letter to JMM, Villa Flora, Menton, 22 February 1920

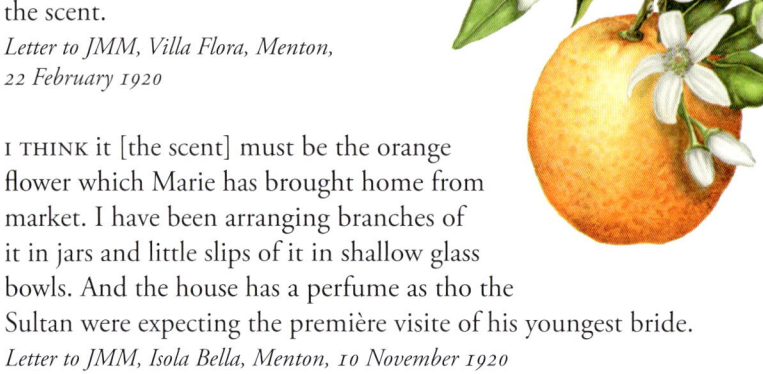

I THINK it [the scent] must be the orange flower which Marie has brought home from market. I have been arranging branches of it in jars and little slips of it in shallow glass bowls. And the house has a perfume as tho the Sultan were expecting the première visite of his youngest bride.
Letter to JMM, Isola Bella, Menton, 10 November 1920

SAW AN ORANGE TREE, an exquisite shape against the sky. When the fruit is ripe the leaves are pale yellow.
Notebook 22 (Notebooks, Volume Two), 5 February 1920

… MY COUSIN [Connie Beauchamp] who has taken this villa for le saison asked me here. *Here* is about as perfect as it could be. A great garden, lemon & orange groves, palms, violets in blue carpets, mimosa trees – and inside a very beautiful 'exquisite' house in the style of Garsington but more sumptuous …
Letter to Richard Murry, Villa Flora, Menton, 24 February 1920

THE ROAD WINDS & winds to get there round & round the mountains. … The rosemary is in flower (our plant it is). The almond trees, pink & white, there are wild cherry trees & the prickly pear white among the olives. Apple trees are just in their first rose & white – wild hyacinths & violets are tumbled out of flora's wicker ark and are *everywhere*. And over everything, like a light are the lemon & orange trees glowing.
Letter to JMM, Villa Flora, Menton, 4 March 1920

BAY LAUREL *Laurus nobilis*

IT IS TOO HOT for any exertion, but a breeze lifts at night – and I can't tell you what scents it brings – the smell of a full summer sea and the bay tree in the garden and the smell of lemons.
Letter to JMM, Isola Bella, Menton, 19 September 1920

LEMON *Citrus limon*

YOUR LITTLE DRAWINGS are most awfully nice. I'll draw you some palms, there are so many different kinds. My favourite tree I really think, tho', is the lemon tree. It's far more beautiful than the orange.
Letter to Richard Murry, Villa Flora, Menton, 13 March 1920

IT IS WINTER NOW – many trees are bare but the oranges, tangerines & lemons are all ripe; they burn in this clear atmosphere – the lemons with gentle flames, the tangerines with bright flashes & the oranges sombre. My tiny peach tree still clings to a few exquisite leaves – curved like peaches – & the violets are just beginning. More and more (for how long? no matter. A moment is for ever) one lives – really lives.
Letter to Dorothy Brett, Isola Bella, Menton, 22 December 1920

PRICKLY PEAR *Opuntia ficus-indica*

AND THEN THE PRICKLY PEAR has a lot of drawing: it's a *very* queer affair & then there's the pepper tree hung of course with pepper pots – but I wish you were here to sneeze at it with me.
Letter to Richard Murry, Villa Flora, Menton, 13 March 1920

AND HERE – I am always sending you greetings – always sharing things with you. I salute you in tangerines and the curved petals of roses thé [tea-roses] and the crocus colour of the sea & in the moonlight on the poire sauvage [prickly pear].
Letter to Anne Rice, Isola Bella, Menton, 26 December 1920

DATURA OR ANGEL'S TRUMPET *Brugmansia aurea*

SO I SLINK AWAY out of sight of everybody, down the steps from the terrace and stand underneath a tree called a datura and there, privately, I gloat. This tree, Sir, is a sight for you. It has small close, grey-green leaves; the buds in their first stage are soft green pods. They open and the flower, tightly folded, springs out and gradually it opens into a long bell-like trumpet about 8 inches long – gold coloured with touches of pale red. But the drawing in the buds and the petals! The gaiety of the edges – the freedom with which Papa Cosmos has let hisself go on them! I have looked at this tree so long that it is transplanted to some part of my brain – for a further transplanting into a story one day.
Letter to Richard Murry, Isola Bella, Menton, 15 November 1920

I have looked at this tree so long that it is transplanted to some part of my brain – for a further transplanting into a story one day.

ROSEMARY *Rosmarinus officinalis*
THYME *Thymus vulgaris*

… THE WILD SPICY SCENT of the rosemary growing in little tufts among the red rocks close to the brim of the sea …
Et in Arcadia Ego

OH DEAR, on the wild hill today I found thyme and rosemary – it reminded me of Bandol in the early morning.
Letter to JMM, Ospedaletti, Italy, 15 October 1919

SPRING, THIS YEAR, is so beautiful that watching it unfold one is filled with a sort of anguish. Why – oh Lord why! I have spent days just walking about or sitting on a stone in the sun and listening to the bees in the almond trees and the wild pear bushes and coming home in the evening with rosemary on my fingers and wild thyme in my toes – tired out with the loveliness of the world.
Letter to Ottoline Morrell, Bandol, France, 22 February 1918

FIG *Ficus carica*

There's a winey smell at the corner of the terrace where a huge fig tree drops its great purple fruits.
Letter to JMM, Isola Bella, Menton, 25 September 1920

MIMOSA (SILVER WATTLE) *Acacia dealbata*

KEZIA LOOKED out through the big bare windows to the wattle trees, their gold tassels nodding in the sunny air, and suddenly the sad tune and the trees moving so gently made her feel quite calm.
Kezia and Tui

I AM ON A LITTLE RISE – to my right a great tree of mimosa laden with blossoms bends & foams in the breeze …
Urewera Notebook (Lake Taupo)

THE PLACE is even to my blind eyes as lovely as ever, glittering with light, with the deep hyacinth blue sea, the wonderful flashing palms and the mountains, violet in the shadow, and jade green in the sun. The mimosa outside my window is in bud …
Letter to JMM, Bandol, France, 11 January 1918

THE DAY is cloudy – but it doesn't matter. Landscape is lovely in this light – it's not like the sea. The mimosa – great puffs of mimosa & great trees of red roses & oranges bright and flashing.
Letter to JMM, L'Hermitage, Menton, 23 January 1920

THE PATH from the gate to the two doors has a big silver mimosa showering across it. The garden is twice as big as I imagined. One can live in it all day.
Letter to JMM, Isola Bella, Menton, 14 September 1920

IT'S 7.15 A.M. and I've just had breakfast in a room lit with great gorse yellow patches of sunlight. Across one patch there's a feathery pattern that dances, that's from the mimosa tree outside.
Letter to Richard Murry, Isola Bella, Menton, 15 November 1920

SUDDENLY through the kitchen window I saw the moon. It was so marvellously beautiful that I walked out of the kitchen door, through the garden … Then I turned round, and the little house faced me – a little white house quivering with light, a house like a candle shining behind a feather of mimosa tree.
Marie and the Cauliflower

COTTON TREE *Gossypium arboreum*

THE COTTON-PODS are huge. Exquisite pale yellow butterflies flutter by …
Letter to JMM, Ospedaletti, Italy, 15 October 1919

I WANT TO OPEN one of those huge great cotton pods with you & see what's inside. I want to discuss the novel with you & to tell you what a darling of darlings you are.
Letter to JMM, Ospedaletti, Italy, 13 November 1919

GRAPE VINE *Vitis vinifera*

IN THE GARDENS the men were cutting grapes. He watched a man standing in the greenish shade, raising up, holding a black cluster in one hand, taking the knife from his belt, cutting, laying the bunch in a flat boat-shaped basket. The man worked leisurely, silently, taking hundreds of years over the job. On the hedges on the other side of the road there were grapes small as berries, growing wild, growing among the stones. He leaned against a wall, filled his pipe, put a match to it …
The Man without a Temperament

HELIOTROPE *Heliotropium arborescens*

SHE HAD HEARD for years of the frightful dangers of the Mediterranean. It was an absolute death-trap. Beautiful, treacherous Mediterranean. There it lay curled before them, its white, silky paws touching the stones and gone again. … But now they were passing a high wall on the land side, covered with flowering heliotrope, and Fanny's little nose lifted. 'Oh George,' she breathed. 'The smell! The most divine …'
Honeymoon

BUT SHE WAS TIRED. She had had enough. She did not want to walk any more.

'Leave me here and go for a little constitutional, won't you? I'll be in one of these long chairs. What a good thing you've got my cape; you won't have to go upstairs for a rug. Thank you, Robert, I shall look at that delicious heliotrope … You won't be gone long?'

'No – no. You don't mind being left?'

'Silly! I want you to go. I can't expect you to drag after your invalid wife every minute … How long will you be?'

… She got up, waved and slowly she came to meet him, dragging the heavy cape. In her hand she carried a spray of heliotrope.

'No, I'm quite all right. Come over here. Sit down by me just a minute, will you, Robert? Ah, that's very nice.' She turned and thrust the piece of heliotrope in the lapel of his coat. 'That,' she said, 'is most becoming.' And then she leaned her head against his shoulder, and he put his arm round her.
The Man without a Temperament

ALMOND *Prunus dulcis*

ONE DAY, ma chère, I pray you share my little Roman villa and I mean to have a blossoming almond tree quivering against a blue sky – and wide, cool rooms lit with daffodils opening their gilded doors to the sunshine which drips through the window vines.
Letter to Vera Beauchamp, Wellington, 12 June 1908

OUTSIDE the sky is light with stars;
There's a hollow roaring from the sea.
And, alas! for the little almond flowers,
The wind is shaking the almond tree.
Camomile Tea

SUCH AIR as you and I have drunk together and a whole flock of little winds to shake every perfumed bud and flower. The almond trees if one stands close & looks up are thick with white and red buds; the lanes have a thick border of white and yellow – wild candytuft and small marigolds.
Letter to JMM, Bandol, France, 24 January 1918

I WALKED to a little valley yesterday that I longed to show you. I sat on a warm stone there: all the almond flowers are gone but the trees are in new leaf and they were full of loving mating birds – quarrelling, you know, about whether to turn the stair carpet under or to cut it off straight. And the trees were playing ball with a little breeze, tossing it to each other –
Letter to JMM, Bandol, France, 28 February 1918

Appendix 1

The influence of *Elizabeth and her German Garden* by Elizabeth von Arnim

> … OUR COUSIN ELIZABETH … appeared today behind a bouquet – never smaller woman carried bigger bouquets. She looks like a garden walking – of asters, late sweet peas, stocks, & always petunias. She herself wore a frock like a spider's web, a hat like a berry and gloves that reminded me of thistles in seed … The point about her is that one loves her and is proud of her.
>
> Letter to Dorothy Brett, Montana-sur-Sierre, Switzerland, 1 October 1921

When she was only ten Kathleen Mansfield Beauchamp read *Elizabeth and her German Garden* by her father's first cousin, Mary Beauchamp, who had married Count von Arnim and lived in Germany. Using the pseudonym 'Elizabeth', the countess wrote about life on her husband's estate. KM saw the book a few months after her own first published story had appeared in the Wellington Girls' College magazine and must have been impressed that she had a near relative who was a successful writer. 'Elizabeth' showed the whole Beauchamp family that writing could be a socially acceptable career. Published in September 1898, *Elizabeth and her German Garden* sold so well that it was reprinted many times in the next few months.

Because KM was very young when she first read *Elizabeth and her German Garden,* it made a deep impression and its influence endured. She was already a keen observer with a superb visual memory, and now she discovered that her cousin was another person who noticed the natural world. *Elizabeth and her German Garden* opened with the sentence, 'I love my garden,' and included detailed descriptions:

> … I lived in a world of dandelions and delights … and under and among the groups of leafless oaks and beeches were blue hepaticas, white anemones, violets, and celandines in sheets … And then … came the lilacs – masses and masses of them … shining glorious against a background of firs.

KM shared, and was encouraged by, this strong love of plants, and continued to observe them through her adolescence. Later she would describe many of

Statue of Elizabeth von Arnim in Buk, Poland.
Wikimedia Creative Commons

them with a few vivid words, with what Mansfield scholar Gerri Kimber called 'the attention to detail that was to be the hallmark of her greatest work.' Her concentration on details was always deliberate. Aged 20, she wrote from London to her lover, Garnet Trowell:

> I like always to have a great grip of Life, so that I intensify the so-called small things – so that truly everything is significant.

Elizabeth and her German Garden was not just another book about a garden — it introduced satire. 'Elizabeth' gently mocks her husband and his power, naming him the 'Man of Wrath'. Ten-year-old KM, already something of a rebel, would have appreciated this humorous jab. She knew how strongly her own father Harold dominated the Beauchamp household: she would later mock *him*.

A third significant idea was suggested by her cousin's book — a visitor to the *German Garden* frequently uses a notebook, explaining that it was:

> … material, you know, for a book. I'm just jotting down what strikes me about your country, and when I have time shall throw it into book form.

This habit became KM's. While still at school, she began to record a variety of jottings, vignettes and drafts of stories in a long succession of notebooks.

In Switzerland in 1921 KM grew to know Elizabeth (now Countess Russell), who was living nearby. She wrote to Dorothy Brett on 25 July 1921:

> She is certainly the most fascinating small human being I have ever known … We exchange books and flowers and fruits. This is a marvellous moment for peaches & apricots & wild strawberries. They grow lower down the mountains. Very little grows here except pines, wild flowers and occasional small bobbing cherries … Every tiny flower seems to shine with a new radiance.

In December 1922 Katherine Mansfield ended a letter to Elizabeth with these words: 'Goodbye, my dearest Cousin. I shall never know anyone like you; I shall remember every little thing about you for ever.'

She died just ten days later.

Jason Mann Photography for Katherine Mansfield House & Garden

Appendix 2

KM's flowers today

KATHERINE MANSFIELD HOUSE & GARDEN

25 Tinakori Road, Thorndon, Wellington.
Open Tuesday to Sunday, 10am–4pm.
www.katherinemansfield.com

Katherine Mansfield was born in this house on 14 October 1888, the same year it was completed. Her father, Harold Beauchamp, had purchased the lease to the land, which ran down to a native bush gully, in 1887. For Harold and his wife Annie, this house was the first step on the social ladder. They would go on to live in much larger houses thanks to Harold's success in business. As a middle-class family on the move, the Beauchamps were committed to presenting themselves as fashionable, modern and confident about the future. Mansfield's memories of the house are captured in *Prelude*, the story which recalls the family's move from Thorndon to Karori in 1893.

For many years it was thought that the house may have been demolished, but research during the 1980s confirmed that the street had been renumbered and Mansfield's birthplace was indeed still standing. The Katherine Mansfield Birthplace Society was formed in 1986 to raise funds to purchase the house, restore its original layout

Katherine Mansfield House & Garden

and open it to the public as a celebration of Mansfield's life, work and creative legacy. The garden was begun in 1988, shortly after the restoration of the house.

The current front garden features plants often seen during Mansfield's lifetime, with an emphasis on those found in her writing, as well as a growing collection of French heritage roses. The back garden is planted with native shrubs and trees to reflect the original landscape. Each year a sale of plants propagated from the garden is held as a popular fundraiser. Katherine Mansfield House & Garden offers a glimpse into the home of a fashionable colonial family, what life was like for Mansfield as a young girl in Wellington, and the life, loves and writing of a woman far away from her first home.

THE MANSFIELD GARDEN AT HAMILTON GARDENS

Hungerford Crescent, Cobham Drive SH1, Hamilton
Open every day, entry free.
www.hamiltongardens.co.nz

Hamilton Gardens, an extremely popular tourist attraction in Waikato, is a national treasure of themed gardens. Its Mansfield Garden represents the early 20th-century New Zealand garden described in *The Garden Party*, with plants, design detail, food and architecture appropriate to the period. There are old-fashioned roses and other exotics fashionable at the time, and the hills behind are planted in natives that grew on the Wellington hills. Other 'Garden Party' touches include the marquee set up on the tennis court against the karaka hedge, with a 'very small band' in a corner of the court — it is as if everything is ready for the party to begin.

Bibliography/works consulted

Antony Alpers, *Katherine Mansfield, A Biography*, Cape, 1954
—— *The Life of Katherine Mansfield*, Viking Press, 1980
Ida Baker, *Katherine Mansfield, The Memories of LM*, Michael Joseph, 1971
Gillian Boddy, *Katherine Mansfield, the woman and the writer*, Penguin, 1988
Laurel Harris, Mary Morris & Joanna Woods (editors), *The Material Mansfield*, Random House, 2008
Gerri Kimber, *Katherine Mansfield: The View from France*, Peter Lang, 2008
—— *Katherine Mansfield: The Early Years*, Edinburgh University Press, 2016
Katherine Mansfield:
—— *Katherine Mansfield, The Aloe*, Vincent O'Sullivan (editor), Carcanet, 1983
—— *Katherine Mansfield: Undiscovered Country, the New Zealand Stories*, Ian Gordon (editor), Longman 1974
—— *Katherine Mansfield's Letters to John Middleton Murry*, Constable, 1951
—— *Poems of Katherine Mansfield*, Vincent O'Sullivan (editor), Oxford University Press, 1988
—— *The Collected Letters of Katherine Mansfield*, five volumes, Vincent O'Sullivan & Margaret Scott (editors), Clarendon Press, Oxford, 1984/87/93/96, 2008
—— *The Collected Poems of Katherine Mansfield*, Gerri Kimber & Claire Davison (editors), Otago University Press, 2016
—— *The Edinburgh Edition of the Collected Works of Katherine Mansfield*, Gerri Kimber, Vincent O'Sullivan, Angela Smith & Claire Davison (editors) Edinburgh University Press, 2012, 2014, 2016
—— *The Journal of Katherine Mansfield*, J Middleton Murry (editor), Constable, 1954
—— *The Katherine Mansfield Notebooks*, Volumes One & Two, Margaret Scott (editor), Lincoln University Press & Daphne Brasell Associates, 1997
—— *The Letters & Journals of Katherine Mansfield: A Selection*, CK Stead (editor), Penguin, 1977
—— *The Urewera Notebook*, Anna Plumridge (editor), Otago University Press, 2015
Ruth Elvish Mantz & J Middleton Murry, *The Life of Katherine Mansfield*, Constable, 1933
Jeffrey Meyers, *Katherine Mansfield: A Biography*, Hamish Hamilton, 1978
Vincent O'Sullivan, *Katherine Mansfield's New Zealand*, Steele Roberts Aotearoa, 2013
Margaret Scott, *Recollecting Mansfield*, Godwit Random House, 2001
Claire Tomalin, *Katherine Mansfield: A Secret Life*, Penguin, 1988

Index of plants

A

agave *Agave americana* 7, 22, 26, 36
almond *Prunus dulcis* 19, 100, 103, 107
aloe *see* agave
anemone *Anemone coronaria* 7, 9-11, 19-20, 108
angel's trumpet *see* datura
antirrhinum *see* snapdragon
apple *Malus domestica* 100
apricot *Prunus armeniaca* 109
aquilegia *see* columbine
arum lily *Zantedeschia aethiopica* 26-27
aster *Asteraceae* 108

B

bamboo *Bambusa vulgaris* 54
bay laurel *Laurus nobilis* 16, 94, 101
bee orchid *see* orchid, bee
beech *Fagus sylvatica* 108
bird cherry *Prunus padus* 25, 59, 109
bluebell *Hyacinthoides non-scripta* 59, 86-88
blue gum *Eucalyptus globulus* 23, 97
boronia *Boronia megastigma* 46
box *Buxus sempervirens* 30, 32
briar/brier rose *Rosa rubiginosa* 57, 81
broom *Cytisus scoparius* 82
bush, New Zealand 73-74, 76-80
bush lawyer *Rubus cissoides* 73, 78
buttercup *Ranunculus repens* 9, 17, 27, 88, 116

C

cabbage tree *Cordyline australis* 37, 67, 73
camellia *Camellia japonica* 31
campion *Silene dioica* 88
Canary date palm *Phoenix canariensis* 38, 62, 95-97, 100-1, 104
candytuft *Iberis sempervirens* 107
canna lily *Canna* 43
Canterbury bells *Campanula* 31
carnation *Dianthus caryophyllus* 10, 48-49, 57, 62, 65, 74, 85 *see also* gillyflower, pink, picotee
celandine *see* lesser celandine
cherry *Prunus avium* 28, 100, 109
chestnut *see* horse chestnut
Christmas rose *Helleborus orientalis* 55
chrysanthemum *Chrysanthemum x morifolium* 65-66, 91
cineraria *Pericallis x hybrida* 46
clematis *Clematis lanuginosa* 7, 47; clematis, NZ *Clematis paniculata* 73, 80
coltsfoot *Tussilago farfara* 59
columbine *Aquilegia vulgaris* 85
convolvulus, pink-flowered bindweed *Calystegia soldanella* 26, 33
cornflower *Centaurea cyanus* 46
cosmos ('cosmia') *Cosmos bipinnatus* 30
cotton tree *Gossypium arboreum* 58, 105
crocus *Crocus vernus* 11, 59, 102

D

daffodil *Narcissus* 43, 45, 85, 98-99, 107
dahlia *Dahlia* 61
damson *Prunus insititia* 116
daisy 7, 9, 14-16, 18, 51-52, 80, 87-88; dog (ox-eye) daisy *Leucanthemum vulgare* 14-15, 18, 52, 80, 87; lawn daisy *Bellis perennis* 9, 14-16, 51, 88, 116
dandelion *Taraxacum officinale* 9, 15-17, 108
daphne *Daphne odora* 52
datura *Brugmansia aurea* 102
double stock *Matthiola incana* 10, 54, 108

E

Eucalyptus *see* blue gum
European silver fir *Abies alba* 17, 63-64, 108
eyebright *Euphrasia officinalis* 88

F

fennel *Foeniculum vulgare* 70
fig *Ficus carica* 45, 103
fir *see* European silver fir
flax *Phormium tenax* 69, 73, 81
forget-me-not *Myosotis sylvatica* 19, 46, 54
foxglove *Digitalis purpurea* 87, 89
freesia/freezia *Freesia* 7, 45, 54
fuchsia *Fuchsia magellanica* 16, 33, 74;
    NZ fuchsia (kotukutuku) *see* konini

G

geranium *see* pelargonium
gillyflower 85 *see also* carnation
golden chain tree *see* laburnum,
gorse *Ulex europaeus* 65, 72, 104
granny bonnet *see* columbine,
grape vine *Vitis vinifera* 105
grape hyacinth *Muscari armeniacum* 54
gum tree *see* blue gum

H

hawthorn (may) *Crataegus monogyna* 45, 83, 85, 92
hazel (nut) *Corylus avellana* 92
heath *Erica* 98
heather *Calluna vulgaris* 89
heliotrope *Heliotropium arborescens* 54, 106
hellebore *Helleborus* 55
hepatica *Hepatica nobilis* 108
holly *Ilex aquifolium* 92
hollyhock *Alcea rosea* 30, 57
honeysuckle *Lonicera japonica* 81
horse chestnut *Aesculus hippocastanum* 48, 60
hyacinth *Hyacinthus orientalis* 25, 43-44, 100, 104
hydrangea *Hydrangea macrophylla* 13, 44

I

iris, flag *Iris pseudacorus* 19, 31, 87, 89
ivy *Hedera helix* 93

J

Japanese sunflower *see* Japanese windflower
Japanese windflower *Anemone hupehensis* 7-8, 32
japonica, flowering quince *Chaenomeles japonica* 48, 62
jasmine *Jasminum* 52

Jerusalem cherry *Solanum pseudocapsicum* 71
jonquil *Narcissus jonquilla* 10, 18, 46, 94, 98-99

K

karaka *Corynocarpus laevigatus* 38, 72-73
konini *Fuchsia excorticata* 73, 80
kowhai *Sophora microphylla* 73

L

laburnum *Laburnum anagyroides* 58, 93
lacebark *Hoheria populnea* 73
laurel *see* bay laurel
lauristinus *see* viburnum
lavender *Lavandula spica* 10, 37-39, 52
lemon *Citrus limon* 16, 94, 100-1
lemon verbena *Aloysia citrodora* 35, 39, 51-52
lesser celandine *Ficaria verna* 62, 108
lilac *Syringa vulgaris* 9, 12-13, 15, 28, 47, 50, 81, 108
lily *see* arum lily, canna lily
lily-of-the-valley *Convallaria majalis* 10
London plane *see* plane
lupin *Lupinus* 85

M

magnolia *Magnolia x soulangeana* 42, 51
mamaku *Cyathea medullaris* 73
manuka *Leptospermum scoparium* 26, 69-70, 73, 75
marigold *Calendula officinalis* 9-10, 18-19, 34-35, 65, 74, 85, 107; French *Tagetes erecta* 9
may *see* hawthorn
Michaelmas daisy *Aster amellus* 91
mignonette *Reseda odorata* 18, 27, 52
mimosa, silver wattle *Acacia dealbata* 10, 100, 104-5
mistletoe, NZ *Peraxilla colensoi* 73, 80
mock-orange *see* orange-ball tree

N

nasturtium *Tropaeolum majus* 33-34, 56-57, 74
nettle *Urtica dioica* 88
nut *see* hazel (nut)

O

oak *Quercus robur* 108
olive *Olea europaea* 98-100
one o'clock *see* dandelion

orange *Citrus sinensis* 18, 95, 100-1, 104
orange-ball tree *Buddleja globosa* 8, 41
orchid: bee orchid *Ophrys apifera* 15;
    sun orchid *Thelymitra* 75

P

palm, palmier *see* Canary date palm
pansy *Viola tricolor* var. *hortensis* 19, 29-30
passion flower/vine *Passiflora caerulea* 7, 40
peach *Prunus persica* 45, 101, 109
pear *Pyrus communis* 42, 48, 55, 93
pelargonium *Pelargonium x hortorum* 6-7, 16,
    34-35, 39, 48, 51-52, 54, 58, 95
peony *Paeonia officinalis* 48, 53
pepper tree *Schinus molle* 102
periwinkle *Vinca* 81
petunia *Petunia x hybrida* 56-57, 108
picotee *Dianthus caryophyllus* 10, 18, 32
pine *Pinus radiata* 16, 40, 65, 68-70
    Pinus sylvestris 17, 22, 63, 68-69, 99, 109
pink 10, 62, 74 *see also* carnation
plane *Platanus x acerifolia* 90
pohutukawa *Metrosideros excelsa* 72, 73
ponga *see* tree fern
poplar, Lombardy *Populus nigra* var. *Italica* 53
poppy *Papaver orientale* 2, 31, 83;
    Papaver rhoeas 14, 28
prickly pear *Opuntia ficus-indica* 100, 102-3
primrose *Primula vulgaris* 9, 55, 59, 85-87
pussy willow *Salix caprea* 45

R

rata: climbing *Metrosideros fulgens* 80;
    tree *Metrosideros robusta* 73, 79-80;
red hot poker *Kniphofia* 32, 81
rhododendron *Rhododendron* 44
rose *Rosa* 9-10, 13, 15, 21-25, 31, 39, 41,
    49-50, 53-54, 58, 81, 85, 98-99, 102,
    104, 110-11
rosemary *Rosmarinus officinalis* 39, 46, 51, 94,
    98, 100, 103

S

sea convolvulus, shore bindweed *Calystegia
    soldanella* 26, 33
sea pink *see* thrift
shore bindweed *see* sea convolvulus
silver fern *see* tree fern

snapdragon *Antirrhinum majus* 31, 56-57, 61
snowdrop *Galanthus nivalis* 26, 43, 93
sorrel *Rumex acetosella* 14
stock *see* Virginia stock, double stock;
    night-scented *Matthiola longipetala* 42
sumac *Rhus typhina* 91
sun orchid *see* orchid, sun
supplejack *Ripogonum scandens* 73, 78-79
sweet pea *Lathyrus odoratus* 57-58, 108
sweet william *Dianthus barbatus* 30-31
syringa *see* lilac

T

tangerine *Citrus tangerina* 24, 46, 97, 101-2
tea tree *see* manuka
thistle *Cirsium vulgare* 108
thorn *see* hawthorn
thrift, sea pink *Armeria maritima* 87
thyme *Thymus vulgaris* 103
toetoe ('toi-toi') *Austroderia fulvida* 7, 73-74
tree fern, silver fern, ponga *Cyathea dealbata*
    73, 77, 79; black tree fern (mamaku)
    Cyathea medullaris 73
tulip *Tulipa* 7, 9, 50-51
tussock *Chionochloa rubra* 75
tutu *Coriaria arborea* 73

V

verbena *Verbena x hybrida* 34-35
viburnum, laurustinus *Viburnum tinus* 47
violet *Viola odorata* 7, 9-11, 20, 25, 30, 59,
    62, 85-87, 98, 100-1, 108
Virginia creeper *Parthenocissus tricuspidata* 91
Virginia stock *Malcolmia maritima* 29

W

wallflower *Erysimum cheiri* 9, 20, 41-42, 54
wattle *see* mimosa
wild strawberry *Fragaria vesca* 109
willow *Salix* 81

X

Xmas rose *see* Christmas rose

Y

yellow monkey flower *Erythranthe guttata* 71

Z

zinnia *Zinnia* 61, 64

COMPILER AND ARTIST

Beverley Randell grew up in Wellington and like KM, walked to Karori School along roads lined with buttercups and daisies. The natural world and small children fascinate her, and she specialises in writing stories for beginners learning to read. Randell Cottage, which Beverley and her husband Hugh Price bought, restored and gifted to the Randell Cottage Writers Trust, was built by her great-grandfather, and is near the Wellington Botanic Garden KM knew so well. Since 2001 it has been a residence for both New Zealand and French writers – reciprocating the Katherine Mansfield Fellowship, which allows New Zealand writers to live and work in Menton.

Jenni Shoesmith, originally from England, moved to Wellington in 2009. A freelance artist and illustrator who uses a variety of media, she has worked in TV and film as a digital artist. Her paintings are largely inspired by nature, depicting real and mythical flora and fauna. Since working on this project, she has been moved by Katherine Mansfield's words and relationship with plants and has become an enthusiastic gardener who talks to her flowers, as she imagines Katherine once did.

No, no, the mind I love must still have wild places –
a tangled orchard where dark damsons drop in the heavy
grass, an overgrown little wood, the chance of a snake
or two (real snakes), a pool that nobody's fathomed the
depth of, and paths threaded with those little flowers
planted by the wind.

('Such a cultivated mind', Notebook 42)